WORSHIP

IS

EXPENSIVE

Ebenezer & Abigail Gabriels

EGE
Ebenezer Gabriels Ministries

Ebenezer & Abigail Gabriels
19644 Club House Road Suite 815
Gaithersburg, Maryland 20886
www.EbenezerGabriels.Org
hello@ebenezergabriels.org

---

www.WorshipIsExpensive.org

ABOUT THE BOOK – WORSHIP IS EXPENSIVE

This book is an experience of who God is in our worship journey. GREAT I AM - That's the Lord and He is set to introduce Himself to the world in this dispensation as the Great I am through worship.

Worship is expensive is more than a book, but an anointed manual for true worshippers who are seeking the worship anointing of old, to get on the journey to find God through worship. It is a manual for those who have drank from polluted streams and are looking for purity from the rivers of living water. WIE is a mission to cultivate deep worshippers whose life will be an uncontaminated source of the presence and power of Yahweh. The Lord is looking for a new breed of fearless and humble believers who are worshippers, who will worship Him in truth and in spirit. He is looking for worshippers who rely on the Holy Spirit 100% to lead them in the way of worship. He is looking for worshippers who are connected to the divine presence of Yahweh, not those who worship to use God for their daily needs .He wants worshippers who will worship Him when there are no guarantees for return on investment. It is easy to worship when there is abundance, when the bans are full, the goats are producing milk, it's easy to lift up hands and say Hallelujah. What happens when there is nothing to hold on or to hang on to? He seeks those who will worship without holding back. Those who will break down before Him in worship.

If your heart is thirsty for God, God is seeking you in worship. If you ever desire to get into uncharted territories in your walk with God, worship is the only place that will lead you there. Worship is expensive is for the thirsty, and for those with the desire to shake vigorously the world, annul earthly spiritual laws to establish Yahweh's desires here on earth. It is a resource for those who desire to plug their life into the source of the stream of God - knowing that downstream is not as pure.

The name of this book is prophetic. The name "Worship is Expensive" is to give the worshipper a deeper insight into the cost of worship. The worshipper whom the Lord seeks is expected to worship Him with the whole heart, body, soul and life inside and outside. A worshipper wears many hats; first they are a worshipper, then they are God's warrior, establishing God's written judgement against God's enemies. Wearing these hats comes from a place of high spiritual authority. Spiritual authority however doesn't come cheap, it comes from the place of total surrender to the Lord, from setting yourself apart for the Lord. Only then, will the director of worship - the Holy Spirit come to dwell with you and take you on a journey of worship.

There is a cluster of God's favorite, they are His worshippers. In the entire world, Israel is known as God's first born, His chosen people - however in Israel, a tribe stands out and that tribe is the tribe of Judah, from where David came and the Lord Jesus Christ. This is the tribe that the worshipper belongs.

Expensive was birthed out of the revelation given to us from many journeys of worship . Y A H W E H has given us the task of raising and restoring worship altars. In fulfilling this mission, we must utterly destroy lesser altars that exalts itself against the altar of the Living God and forbids God's people from worshipping Yahweh.

Worship is Expensive as a book is the revelation of worship, the history of worship, the exploration of true worshippers as revealed to us by the Lord. As a mission, this book summons readers into building highly flammable worship altars for Yahweh.

Worship is sacred, and carries a potent explosives that is yet unaccessed by our generation. The Lord said my husband and I , "Show them, pour it all out, lay it bare, all that I have shown you in the past 4 years of your worship walk with me". How Lord? "I will teach you, I will show you". And here we are, showing you some of the priceless experiences what the Lord has shown us. Let's begin.

Lord, how can we bring them knowing that the price of worship is expensive ? Yes, worship is indeed expensive, but the glory in worship is priceless. Then we asked why now? We are entering into the phase of the visibility of His glory here on earth. But we must count the cost of worship.

TABLE OF CONTENTS

Section I - Origins of Worship & War Against Worship

Section II - Exploration into the Hearts of Worshippers

Section III - Journeying into the Depths of Worship

SECTION ONE

THE ORIGINS OF WORSHIP & THE WAR AGAINST WORSHIP

1

EXPLORING WORSHIP

We may put collections of beautiful notes together. We may arrange fine words or make rhythmic sounds, if it is not pleasing to God, it is not considered worship. Worship is as a journey to the worshipper, traveling in the Spirit with one destination in mind - the heart of the Father. Worship could be words, music, lifestyle or actions - but worship is not music. Whenever a person rises up and determines in their hearts that they are going to depart from the noise of the world and offer worship to Yahweh, God's heart is pleased and every of their action if may be counted as worship before the King of kings.There is a deeper deep in worship than any other deep. The deeper depths of worship, the lower lows of worship, the highest highs of worship can only be experienced when one is totally surrendered to the spirit of the world. Worship is a journey into the heart of the Father. The heart of the Father is vast. The Lord takes some through a different entry into His heart, taking some miles into His heart, giving some mile zero into their hearts, because it is the director of worship that navigates the worshipper that navigates through the heart of the Father. You see some people just get torn apart in worship

God is spirit, Jesus alerted us. If God is spirit, how then do we worship God? What then is worship? Worship is impossible to fit into the written or verbal expression because it is a dynamic experience.

Worship has already been in ancient times before us. When the genealogy of Jesus was written, if we bring into remembrance the lives of worshippers explored in the Scriptures, we would understand how they entered into the realm of worship, and have a vision of the ministry of the worshipper. The world has been preserved through the intercession arising from the heart of worshippers.

The Scripture illuminates the subject of worship through the lives of people whose sacrifices became a sweet, pleasing and delightful memorial to the Lord. To help us understand worship, the Lord reveals sweet-smelling aroma as a noteworthy essence of true and acceptable worship. As a perfumer creates desirable scents by mixing the right spices and oil together, so does the worshipper prepares a mixture of praises and sacrifices to God which translates into worship before the Lord. No worshipper knows for sure what these recipes are, but the worshipper knows that absolute holiness, the word of God are major ingredients, and places reliance on the directions from the Holy Spirit to offer true and acceptable worship to the Lord.

Jesus gave the format of worship. He said, *"But the hour is coming, and now is, when the true worshipers will worship the Father in spirit and truth; for the Father is seeking such to worship Him"*-John 4:23 NKJV. Verses leading to this major subject talks about a woman who brings the subject of worship back from history to the current time. This woman had questions about worship. She had questions about the location of worship because there seems to be a difference in beliefs. Jesus admits that timing is essential to the way worship is done.

What Makes Up Worship?

The Worshipper
A worshipper is similar to a perfumer, the one who creates perfumes. The worshipper is a creator of pleasing fragrances to the Lord as sacrifices. A worshipper can be compared to a perfumer who

specializes in mixing spices and oils together to produce signature scents. The perfumer is tasked with mixing the right spices and oils to produce desirable fragrances. This is made possible by some knowledge of perfume production that the perfumer has. Similarly, the worshipper is a vessel, who uses the right recipe to make sweet fragrances with pleasing aroma to the Lord. However, the worshipper cannot do this by themselves, they rely solely on the direction of the Holy Spirit for guidance on the way to worship God. . A worshipper is distinguished from all others by the worship they have in them. The worship in a person is marked by their sacrifice for God.

Worship

Worship is like s a fragrance. Worship is like the end product of the creation of the perfumer. All nicely prepared and ready to be taken over by the consumer. Worship is the aroma, the end product that goes to please and delight the Lord. An acceptable worship is delightful to the Lord. God loves our worship. Worship is so important to God that He never shares the glory of His worship with anyone. No wonder the fastest way satan ruins the lives of people is to tempt them to share in God's glory. Worship, all that is called worship is only reserved for God. We are not to partake in it.

The Holy Spirit

God is not boxed up in a worship session. We cannot say, this is how we worshipped God yesterday, so let's do the same today. Worship does not occur in a template. Worship has the attribute of currency. Worship is timely. Worship is topical, worship happens based on current events ongoing in the heart of God. A seasoned worship leader who thinks his experiences can lead others into worship fails woefully at his thought. The Holy Spirit is the director of worship who leads the production of worship. For worship to occur, the Holy Spirit has to be involved, and take the lead..

Truth

The world is such a strange place, a place where the truth is suppressed for untruth. We live in a world where the truth attracts enmity, and lies breeds friendships. Rosemary is a deaconess at a local church. Rosemary is described as one of the meekest persons by people who know her. However, when Rosemary is not in public view, Rosemary's lies to cover up her shortcoming. When asked why she lies despite her status in the church, Rosemary, was not remorseful and continues to live in sin. Jesus is the only source of truth. Truth cannot flow from outside of Jesus. Worship cannot also occur outside of truth. Worship can only be offered to the Lord when we live in the truth of Jesus. The brutal truth of Jesus makes us realize that regardless of how far we have strayed, salvation is still available while we live. Worship cannot take place without the living in the truth of Jesus. The truth of Jesus is a vital part of worship

The Father

God does not seek to keep us in a mysterious relationship with Him. He wants worshippers to know Him and relate with Him as a personal and approachable Father. He wants us to learn about Him. Many worship God from a far and strange place. The worshipper must know the Father. The worshipper must get to know who He is that we worship. Many offer worship without thinking about where their worship is going. The worshipper must have one goal in mind, to offer God alone worship. Satan seeks to make the destination of worship blurry, he often succeeds when worshippers do not take time to seek the Lord. Yahweh, is the only One to worship. In the upcoming chapters, we will study how satan lures worshippers out of God's presence, by subtly diverting their worship. Let's look at how worship was in times past during the times of the law and how it has evolved since the coming of the Lord Jesus.

2

HEAVENS OF HEAVENS

Worship originated from Yahweh's dwelling place in Heaven. The vastness of the glory in Yahweh's presence places the creatures around in Him in a perpetual state of awe spurring unending worship. Heaven is the kingdom of endless worship of Yahweh by thousands times thousands of His heavenly hosts. In heaven, worship never stops or pauses. Every creator, known and unknown to man stands at their duty post, worshipping the Lord. Heaven is the purest of all places - it is where worship never ceases.

The Lamb of God

Starting from the Lord Jesus, He heard His famous title, "Lamb of God" because of the rarest form of worship that He offered to the Lord. His costly worship has earned Him exaltation and a very powerful name.A seat of the highest honor, at the right hand of God was granted to a man like no other which the Son of the Living God attained through worship. Jesus continues to minister worship in heaven.

16

The 24 Elders

Around the throne of Yahweh are some dignitaries in the kingdom of God. They are numbered twenty-four. They are no ordinary men. They are of greater ages - they are called "elders". They are of noble ranks; not in this world, not in the darkness, but in the glorious presence of God. They are highly-decorated and endowed with authority, appareled in white robes and adorned in crowns of gold. The twenty-four elders reflects the model of true worship in leadership. Their status, class, state is of no repute when it is time to worship Yahweh.

They are the council of elders in heaven. We may not fully understand the roles of these elders, but one thing is certain, thrones are seats of power, and no powerless person sits on a throne, yet these powerful elders submit themselves to the King of kings in worship. To think that the other 24 elders who put aside their crowns to worship God, and that these elders have their throne around God's, and perhaps a part of the court session is part of the mysteries of worship in heaven.

The Cherub & Seraph

The Seraphim are the fiery angelic beings standing above the throne of Yahweh. These are six-winged angels. Because of the abundance of glory in the presence of the Lord and these beings cannot behold His glory; they cover their faces and feet in God's presence. They worship the Lord day and night saying *"Holy, holy, holy is the Lord of hosts; the whole earth is full of his glory!*

The Cherubim are the four-faced angelic angels by the throne of God. In between the Cherubim is where the dwelling place of the Lord. The Cherub are also said to cover the mercy seat. The Cherubim solely exist to worship and stay close to the throne of Yahweh. Because of their proximity to the Lord and they are also all covered up in God's presence. Lucifer belonged to the group of angels called the Cherubs.

There are millions and millions of angels, for God's several purposes. Angels are fierce worshippers, and man is not to give worship to angelic beings. All worship must go to the Lord.

The Court & The Seat of Justice

On a certain day I was in prayers and the Spirit of God led me to a prayer of judgement against God's enemies who would not not repent, but continue in wickedness. As I closed my eyes and opened my mouth, decreeing justice from God's court, I saw a door opened, with the arrangement of chairs. Fear gripped me, and the Lord said to me, "the courts in heaven was in session". Thinking about this afterwards, my mind raced to Daniel 7 where Daniel saw the court seated in heaven and the books were opened. And here's what I saw;

Daniel 7:9-10 NKJV

I watched as thrones were put in place and the Ancient One sat down to judge.His clothing was as white as snow, his hair like purest wool. He sat on a fiery throne with wheels of blazing fire, and a river of fire was pouring out, flowing from his presence. Millions of angels ministered to him; many millions stood to attend him. Then the court began its session, and the books were opened.

Heaven is where the highest court is. It is where God's judgement seat is, and where all justice is pronounced. Unlike earthly courts where justice is imperfect by the one imperfect man judging another imperfect man, the justice system is far above that which we see here. Worship precedes the court session. Millions and millions of angels minister worship to the Father. Worshipping Him in the highest possible levels of holiness, truth and spirit. Here, there is no impure thing or person. There is no bias, no injustice, no corruption or pollution. In heaven, holiness which gives no room for an iota of impurity is an attribute of God's justice.

The Foe: A Former Insider

Lucifer was no stranger to God's throne room. Satan was previously positioned as a lead Cherub; suggesting he was at a close proximity to the throne of God. Not only that; he knew the intricacies of worship in Heaven.   He was an anointed Cherub; and he was all covered up in the presence of God. He was the archangel amidst the multitude of worshippers of God in Heaven; he was finely and exquisitely created. In place of skin, he had fine topaz, diamond, onyx, jasper, sapphire, turquoise, the mix of emerald and gold as his covering. He was a master worship crafter. A range of new skills with which satan worshipped were equally created at his inception. His shine was so bright that he was called *the morning star*. To put that into perspective; stars only come out at night. A star which shines beyond the night into the morning is a dazzling glitter. Lucifer was the definition of perfection.

The anointed Cherub worshipped created sweet worship unto Yahweh until leaven was found in him; fermenting the worship he offered and reducing it to profanity. In Him was found many vices; iniquity, defilement, internal violence, profanity, corrupted wisdom and pride. He was singled out for destruction, thrown out of the most Holy place, of the presence of the Lord. Lucifer enjoyed his former position; and wanted to be elevated into the position of the Lord. He wanted to become the recipient of worship. Unashamed of his ruin, he deployed a host of rogue angels to go along with him in his newly established kingdom on earth. Some of these fallen angels; he's made princes over regions of the nations of the earth.

Mankind, The Enemy & Pirated Worship

Man was made with earth materials that in no way compares to the fine sapphires and topaz as well as other precious metals that covers the devil. Man was made from dust. Satan fails to understand why he would be replaced with beings created from inexpensive materials and how the worship of man would delight Yahweh so much. Since the creation of mankind; Satan has fought against man's call to worship the Lord. He has succeeded in creating pirated worship, counterfeit thrones and wicked altars.

Lucifer knows that consecration was standard in Heaven; but his earthly worship institution teaches that holiness is no longer a prerequisite to worship the Holy Lord in Heaven. Unlike Heaven's worship company where admission is highly competitive and selective. Admission to Satan's worship institute is quite cheap and pretty easy to obtain. In place of holiness; Satan's offers people unholiness, he sells iniquity and markets profanity. He counters every nudging of the Holy Spirit with the wrong usage of the Scriptures. Admission-seekers enter en mass because the offer looks promising and harmless. Having a wealth of experience in worship; Lucifer knows what constitutes an abomination against the Lord. The fallen Cherub who is now the archenemy of human worshippers created to replace him before God. All he simply does is to lead worshipers away from the Lord tactfully. He is well aware that any worship not going to Adonai is coming to Him. Here's why we see many worship which were originally intended for Yahweh get perverted because the worshippers submitted to the inspiration of the archenemy.

How does God tell when worship is polluted? It comes as a stench to Him because *The spirit of a man is the lamp of the Lord,Searching all the inner depths of his heart* - Proverbs 20:17. How does Lucifer pervert worshippers from the worship of Yahweh? How does he enter into the hearts of men to divert worship to himself? It all started in Eden.

3

MOLDED TO WORSHIP

God is not predictable. He chose man to often does so by choosing those who are not expected to be chosen. When man was chosen to worship God. He chose man from properties that were not desired.   When all other celestial properties were created from precious stones and fire, man was created with clay -too give worship. In worship, God gives no room to pride whatsoever, so we do not think we are fit to worship because we have the right set of skills or talents. In worship, there is a new realm of God's glory opened up to worshippers where people that have been termed as "nonentities become acceptable vessels of worship, where the shame, oppressed and neglected become cornerstones. In this realm of glory in worship is where power is released to the seemingly unqualified, and an anointing for worship is released. This was the case for mankind. When lucifer was thinking his replacement in worship would be another archangel made with shining lights, man was molded from dust.

Eden

Eden was planted by God for man. In Eden was fertile soil,

stable environment, the right temperature, abundance of water supply - everything from the climate to the crops planted were all in perfect condition. Adam didn't have to pay for the price of Eden - he didn't need to search for a land to use or purchase for farming. He didn't need to check if there was any government regulations on the land if he were going to purchase it. He also did not have to worry about getting raw materials and farming equipment. He did not need to conduct a market research to determine the demand for his production. He didn't need to minimize air or water pollution, he had no need for pest control, he had none of the needs that came with farming.

Genesis 2:8-9 NKJV

The Lord God planted a garden eastward in Eden, and there He put the man whom He had formed. And out of the ground the Lord God made every tree grow that is pleasant to the sight and good for food.

Eden – A Place To Thrive

In Eden were vibrant trees. Trees that grew in conditions that are impossible to find in modern days. Out of all the trees; there was one in Eden that was the envy of others. It produced fine branches, had underground waters watering it from its roots, beautiful in length and breath, fine in branches and high in its heights. The Scriptures below shares more:

Ezekiel 31:2-9 NKJV

Whom are you like in your greatness? Indeed Assyria was a cedar in Lebanon, With fine branches that shaded the forest, And of high stature; And its top was among the thick boughs. The waters made it grow; Underground waters gave it height, With their rivers running around the place where it was planted, And sent out rivulets to all the trees of the field. 'Therefore its height was exalted above all the trees of the field; Its boughs were multiplied, And its branches became long because of the abundance of water, As it sent them out.All the birds of the heavens made their nests in its boughs; Under its branches all the beasts of the field brought forth their young; And in its shadow all great nations made their home. 'Thus it was beautiful in greatness and in the length of its branches,Because its roots reached to abundant waters. The cedars in the garden of God could not hide it;The fir trees were not like its boughs, And the chestnut trees were not like its branches; No tree in the garden of God was like it in beauty. I made it beautiful with a multitude of branches, So that all the trees of Eden envied it, That were in the garden of God.

Adam's life in Eden was like a life planted by the rivers of water. The trees which produced his food brought forth its fruits on time and he was prosperous in all he did. The branch of the trees he cared for were green and leafy, he never had a reason to worry about drought.

Worship: Man's Primary Purpose

The Prophet Ezekiel shared about this tree which reveals the privileges of nature given to Adam in Eden. Adam didn't need to plant. He didn't need to worry about growth. He only needed to nurture what had been placed in his care. Genesis 2:15 points out that the Lord placed Adam in Eden *to tend* and *to keep* it followed with the instructions to stay away from eating the tree of the knowledge of good and evil.

Man was made with creativity. And in man was found creativity. Man's creativity was the first thing God put to test. Genesis 2:19-20 - *Out of the ground the Lord God formed every beast of the field* *and every bird of the air, <u>and brought them to Adam to see what he would</u>* <u>*call them.*</u> *And whatever Adam called each living creature, that was its name. So Adam gave names to all cattle, to the birds of the air, and to every beast of the field. But for Adam there was not found a helper comparable to him.* This was man's first test, and he passed the creativity test. God tested the creativity in Adam; and he delighted the Lord. This was man's test. Who ever knew working in creativity is as worship unto the Lord? His creativity in giving every animal reveals the gifts of specificity in Adam. He knew what to give to who. After naming the animals, the Lord was moved to create a helper for Adam; one whom will be joined to him to continue to delight the Lord.

Walking in our giftings is a form of worship. Using diligently the gifts that has been placed in our lives delights the Lord and it comes up to Him as pleasure. In our mortal states as men, which of us creates something beautiful and would not be filled with joy when our creations work just fine? Every one of God's creations, the sun, the moon and the stars in fulfilling their assignments worship the Lord. Let's learn how.

The Trees: Made to Worship

I came to learn that a man in honor who knows it not is as a perishing beast. Take a look at the parables of the trees;

Judges 98-15 (CJB)

Once the trees went out to choose a king to rule them. They said to the olive tree, 'Rule over us!' But the olive tree replied, 'Am I supposed to leave my oil, which is used to honor both God and humanity, just to go and hold sway over the trees?' So the trees said to the fig tree, 'You, come and rule over us!' But the fig tree replied, 'Am I supposed to leave my sweetness and my good fruit just to go and hold sway over the trees?' So the trees said to the grapevine,

'You, come and rule over us!' But the grapevine replied, 'Am I supposed to leave my wine, which gives cheer to God and humanity, just to go and hold sway over the trees?' Finally, all the trees said to the thorn bush, 'You, come and rule over us!' The thorn bush replied, 'If you really make me king over you, then come and take shelter in my shade. But if not, let fire come out of the thorn bush and burn down the cedars of the L'vanon!'

If the fig tree catches the revelation of worship; if the Olive tree understand that in producing oil it worships the Lord or if the grapevine knows that its vine which cheers the Lord is as worship unto Him - how can man be ignorant that the Lord wants to impute every of his daily task as worship unto Him?

All Creatures & Creations Worship

Not one of His creations is exempted from worship. The sun, moon, stars, waters, and even the heavens are called to worship. The animals, all of them, sea creatures, land creatures, flying and creeping animals. Fire, hail, snow, cloud, and all the people, both low and High, young and old and infants worship the Lord. The sun comes out every morning in full strength its place of assignment to provide light for God's people. In the evening, the sun goes back to its chambers after fulfilling that which has been sent for the day.

All creations are ordained worshipers ministering worshipping worship to the Lord.

Adam's Failings

Adam though insightful and brilliant was not diligent in keeping that revelation of worshipping through His giftings and submissions to instructions. Adam soon came face-to-face with the farmer's dilemma where he soon realizes that a man who lacks diligence becomes careless with instructions and will eventually pay for it for the rest of his life. Mankind's privileges to such abundance in life; spiritually, physically, mentally, emotionally is restored when man returns to the truest state of worship. He had an abundance of water supply watering the crops. It was grown for man. Adam didn't need to plant, he only needed to go out

The Sun, The Moon, The Stars, The Earth, The Trees and all other Creations

The reason why we discuss the worship of the hosts of Heaven unto the Lord is to create awareness that humans are not the only being called to worship the Lord. We must ensure that we never worship any of God's creation. It is easy to have this revelation and fall into error of worshipping them. Only Yahweh is to be worshipped.The sun is an ordained minister of God. The sun was enacted by the very word of God. The moon is a minister of God. Why couldn't they cover the glory of sun forever because they are thriving, it is not possible. The sun will not agree with them and say you are a minister, and I am a minister... show me your credentials... The person that the Lord gives through access can say dont change duties yet... until I am through with the works of God.by the order of the Lord. Yet some worship the sun and the moon not knowing they are ministers. Yet the ones God created with His hand, and put HIs breathes into do not understand the authority into their lives.

4

WORSHIP, FOUNDATIONS & SPIRITUAL WAR

Without resolving foundational problems, worship will be easily perverted and profaned. Worship is a superlative weapon of warfare. With worship, no true worshipper of Yahweh can be defeated in any kind of warfare. A worshipper holds many two privileges in spiritual warfare. The first is that the Lord Himself does the fighting, and the worshipper is given prophetic privileges. There's nothing as dangerous and potent to the enemy than the worshipper who identifies worship as a major spiritual battle machinery. Anytime any of God's name is called upon in worship, the function of that name is fulfilled in the name of Yahweh. The Lord makes a name for Himself in the life of the worshipper.The devil will do everything, including tearing apart lives, families and destinies to prevent through worship.

The only way to go is a foundational warfare.

Spiritual warfare precedes worship. In our foundations is idolatry. There is none exempted. Since the moment satan was cast out of Heaven, entering into the realm of true worship for mankind has been tough. No other thing except worship paves the way into the presence of God. Since mankind lost access to God's presence at Eden; the devil continues to look for ways to keep people locked out.

Covenants of the Foundations

Adam was placed in Eden to care for the beautiful garden of God! Who ever knew that diligently doing the job that God entrusts in our care is as worship unto Him. God gave Adam the gifts of creativity - "*Out of the ground the Lord God formed every beast of the field and every bird of the air, and brought them to Adam to see what he would call them. And whatever Adam called each living creature, that was its name.* - Genesis 2:10. How delighted God was to see the creation he has made king over all other creations come up with such creativity in naming all other creations. That pleased the Lord and God made Adam a special helper, so they could work together to delight the Lord further. There was a cunning one who was a former insider in God's presence who understood that obedience is imputed as worship and disobedience jeopardizes the worshipper. In his deceitfulness, satan lured the woman and by extension the man who also bowed and submitted to the devil's offer; giving satan the honor of obedience which is a form of worship that belongs to only Adonai. From that moment, idolatry entered into our foundations; and all men and women as long as they are descendants of Adam and Eve have a history of idolatry. Idolatry holds God's people back from worshipping Him. Idolatry puts people away from the Lord's presence. Idolatry fights brutally against worship.

Abel

The first true worshipper ever to be recorded in the Scriptures was Abel. Abel was a shepherd whose offering received the favor of the Lord. For His worship unto the Lord, his brother despised him and murdered him. From the time of Abel to the time of Noah, we never heard about any worshipper in between them.

Many desire to worship the Lord, but that desire never pass the idea stage before the enemy sieves them away. Satan's sole mission is to lock up people under terrible affliction which he expects them to nurse for the rest of their lives to prevent them from worshipping. This is why idolatry is deeply rooted in oppression. There is no oppressed person who will be able to worship God wholeheartedly. When satan assigns people filthy task, as their taskmaster, he ensures close supervision to ensure they never slip out or ever think of worshipping God.

This is why the foundational deliverance precedes true worship. Idolatry is the chain keeping many in bondage today. When we realize that worship is the greatest weapon of warfare that brings the utmost form of deliverance. To enter into utmost freedom and power that comes with worship; we must fight hard for it. We begin to approach the subject of worship differently. Our human foundations has strayed from the worship of the Lord right from Eden. Anyone who would successfully break free from the worldly order of satan needs to be delivered from the foundation.

Any worshipper whose outlook of worship is based on themselves, their attitude, their willingness to worship is far from the truth. How do you explain a person who desires to worship the Lord and is met with afflictions that seek to take away their focus from worship? How do you explain a person who makes up their mind to worship the Lord only to fall into adultery? How can you tell of a person whose intention is to worship but only find out that they are motivated to promote self when they get in front of God's people whom they were supposed to lead into worship?

Covenants of the Foundations

In our foundations is idolatry. There is none exempted. Adam and Eve surrendered to the devil's offer; and gave Satan the honor of obedience, a form of worship which belongs to only Adonai.

When the beloved lift up their voices in worship, the kingdom of darkness tremble. They become restless During Israel's captivity in Egypt. God sent Moses to Pharaoh *tell Pharaoh to let my people go so they can worship me* in Exodus 9:1. Prior to a person's entry into true worship, there is a foreign god reign.

Gideon: Worship & Warfare

In Gideon's story, the Scriptures brings forth the revelation of spiritual warfare in worship. Every worshipper needs to be aware that the desire to worship Yahweh alone is not enough; spiritual war against the forces of darkness that seeks to hinder true worship is paramount.

Gideon: Worship As a Witness

At a time when Israel was under the captivity of the Midianites was when Gideon lived. Gideon and the Israelites were under such a huge oppression that their hard-earned food produce constantly hot destroyed by the oppressors. After a national cry; the Lord attended to them.

All odds were against Gideon. His tribe was the weakest. There was little or no history of winning wars recorded in the clan of Manasseh. Whenever Israel goes to war and men of valor were selectively placed in warfronts, it was highly unlikely THAT a man from Gideon's tribe would feature. called to lead because it highly unlikely unlikely for them to defeat the enemy. Gideon came from this tribe. That was not only Gideon's challenge. Gideon was also not the first child, he was the least of his father's. The Lord spins a surprise on Gideon saying: *Go in this might of yours, and you shall save Israel from the land of the Midianites - Judge 6:26.*

A worshipper's first instinct is never to receive from God; but to give to God. Gideon asked for the uncommon; He demanded more of God's time as he goes to prepare to worship God knowing that worship always comes as a witness between God and man.

Gideon's Request →

Judges 6:18 NIV

*Please do not go away until I come
back and bring my offering and set
it before you." And the LORD said,
"I will wait until you return."*

Gideon came all prepared to worship the Lord. For every genuine worship directed to Yahweh; a sign follows.

Judges 6:19-21 NKJV

So Gideon went in and prepared a young goat, and unleavened bread from an ephah of flour. The meat he put in a basket, and he put the broth in a pot; and he brought them out to Him under the terebinth tree and presented them. The Angel of God said to him, "Take the meat and the unleavened bread and lay them on this rock, and pour out the broth." And he did so. Then the <u>Angel of the Lord put out the end of the staff that was in His hand, and touched the meat and the unleavened bread; and fire rose out of the rock and consumed the meat and the unleavened bread.</u> And the Angel of the Lord departed out of his sight.

After he presented his offerings before the Angel of God, and fire consumed His sacrifice; Gideon was able to establish that as a proof that God was the one who communicated with him and promised to deliver Israel from captivity through his hands.

Gideon: The Worshipper As a BattleAxe

Once a worshipper is set aside and chosen as a worshipper; they no longer have control over the cause of their lives. Every worshipper of the Lord is commissioned as a battle ax of Yahweh the day they set their hearts to worship. As a vessel of worship, they also become a warring tool for God. When a worship offering is accepted; the presence of God comes to abide in the place and every existing altar of other gods and evil presence are extinguished. After Gideon built an altar which he called *The-Lord-is-Peace*. The Lord revealed unto Gideon the altar of Baal of his father's household.The Lord opened up this revelation to expose the satanic altars in his foundation that would hinder him as a worshipper, as a warrior of the Lord and in his assignment.

Judges 6:25-29 NKJV

Now it came to pass the same night that the Lord said to him, "Take your father's young bull, the second bull of seven years old, and tear down the altar of Baal that your father has, and cut down the wooden image that is beside it; and build an altar to the Lord your God on top of this rock in the proper arrangement, and take the second bull and offer a burnt sacrifice with the wood of the image which you shall cut down." So Gideon took ten men from among his servants and did as the Lord had said to him. But because he feared his father's household and the men of the city too much to do it by day, he did it by night.

Any worshipper who has not undergone foundational deliverance will be pulled back by the strings of demonic influences of family idols. If there's an evil altar where your blood is soul is still tied, if there's a demonic altar still holding the control of your spirit and you have not not shattered the hold of those altars over your life; the dark powers from those altars will stop you.

Idols and The Foundations
We listened to an individual who sang a song. It was well put together and the lyrics looked good. While we were thinking of how

different it was and seemingly nice. God spoke to us and said, "the applause of the crowd is never the measure of a person's spiritual standing with Me". The Lord further said, "the individual who sang the song has deep roots of Sango (*an African god - the god of thunder*) in their foundations. There is also the presence of another god called obatala buried in their foundation. If unchecked, that idol will stop them from getting into true worship and where the Lord wants them to get with Him. When those deities are left unchallenged, they show up in the mannerism of their captives. They hinder the delivery of the word of God in worship. As the singer sang, a lot of demonic transference was taking place and the demonic deities were hidden during the performance from those who lacked the spirit of discernment.

This demonic deity called sango is the god who comes across as an angry god; it's also synonymous with fire and power amongst its worshippers. In the Yoruba culture, the spirit tries to present itself at the Holy Spirit. They fashioned the deity in the similitude of the Holy Spirit and attempts to copy the trait of the Holy Spirit which is where the fire and power idea came from. Any vessel with this spirit of the deity of sango in them can be mistaken as a worshipper if care is not taken. In their lives will be deep and unresolved anger issues. They wreck more havoc than good and taint the gospel. There are a lot them leading crowds at gospel events, yet they are entrenched in this demonic deity and this demonic god hiding behind the facade uses the vessels to reach and spread demonic infestations to many during concerts. When ignorant people see the manifestation of the sango spirit during worship, they think they have been touched with the Holy Spirit. Rather than having their yokes broken during worship, their chains are refastened and harder.

Gideon's Unfinished War on Idols

An *Ephod is* a priestly garment described by the Lord in Scriptures to Moses. Moses was given the pattern and material specifications for the design of the priestly *Ephod*. It is clear that every item used in the worship of Yahweh at the time was hand-picked by Yahweh Himself, no wonder why He warned Moses to ensure he builds according to the pattern shown to Him. In one instance, the Lord said to Moses in Exodus 28:39, "You shall make the robe of the *ephod* all of blue. There was another instance in Exodus 29:5, *the Lord specified how the Ephod was to be worn on the High Priest.*

"Then you shall take the garments, put the tunic on Aaron, and the robe of the ephod, the ephod, and the breastplate, and gird him with the intricately woven band of the ephod"

Our obedience in following the pattern of worship given to us by the Lord. If it were not, He would not make us in His own copy. He would not expect us to be like Him.

Worshippers, especially those who are first generation worshippers of Yahweh coming out of idolatry must never be deceived into thinking that their deliverance is a one-off experience. When demons are cast out of a place, they will always come back at a later time to check for openness. If they are given access, they come back stronger. Here is why it is harder to deliver a person who had undergone deliverance initially and went back to open up the gateways to their lives to the devil. More violent demons are brought in. In Gideon's situation, the people sought to worship him, and he yielded. He requested for the jewelry of the Israelites, these jewelries were plundered from the Ishamelites. The Ishmaelites came out of Ismael, the son of Abraham from Hagar. When God told Abraham to listen to his wife and send the foreign woman (Hagar) and her son (Ishmael) away, because they were not destined to become Israel, the nation of God, they were the ones who went ahead to become the Arab nation today. From the plunders of the Ishmaelites did Gideon tell the people to donate gold which would be used in making an Ephod. It was not an ephod for God, it was made of foreign materials. Whenever the pattern given by God is altered and a foreign recipe is introduced, God departs. Immediately, the gold earrings and other jewelry were made into an ephod and Gideon lifted it up in his city and all Israel worshipped the ephod. The Scripture records *"It became a snare to Gideon and his house"*- *Judges 8:27b*. The idol turned the heart of an entire nation back to the devil. How did a man who was hungry for God became ensnared? He opened up the door to an idol in his foundation.

Covenant of the Foundations

In our foundations is idolatry. There is none exempted. Adam and Eve surrendered to the devil's offer; and gave Satan the honor of obedience, a form of worship which belongs to only Adonai. From then till this moment; everyone is held back from worshipping God in truth by their foundation until they are delivered.

After the death of David, in the beginning of His reign; Solomon did not get to work immediately. He went to Gibeon to the bronze altar to sacrifice a thousand animals to the Lord in worship. When we convert the cost and time it took him to worship the Lord, we are looking at tens of thousands of dollars today. That worship session was quite an expensive one! Solomon worshipped away, not hindered by the cost.

In all the vastness of the wisdom God gave to Solomon; the devil didn't seek to lure him out of prominence, but out of worship. Why? He had not dealt with the rottenness in his foundation. A righteous person is one who under grace is living rightfully, and keeping their hearts to the word of the Lord, and following the footsteps of Jesus. We cannot be righteous by our own works, but righteousness can be inputted unto us through acts of faith, worship and service, amongst other goodness empowered by grace.

Solomon was the one given the grace to build the temple for God. A task that the Lord didn't give his father David. Solomon followed closely the patterns given to Moses in building. Solomon also followed closely the instructions of his father David;

2 Chronicles 14-15 ESV

"According to the ruling of David his father, he appointed

the divisions of the priests for their service, and the Levites for

their offices of praise and ministry before the priests as the duty of each day required, and the gatekeepers in their divisions at each gate, for so David the man of God had commanded. And they did not turn aside from what the king had commanded the priests and Levites concerning any matter and concerning the treasuries".

That night after worship, this conversation took place between Solomon and God in a dream;

2 Chronicles 1:4-12 ESV Version

In that night God appeared to Solomon, and said to him, "Ask what I shall give you." And Solomon said to God, "You have shown great and steadfast love to David my father, and have made me king in his place. O Lord God, let your word to David my father be now fulfilled, for you have made me king over a people as numerous as the dust of the earth. Give me now wisdom and knowledge to go out and come in before this people, for who can govern this people of yours, which is so great?" God answered Solomon, "Because this was in your heart, and you have not asked for possessions, wealth, honor, or the life of those who hate you, and have not even asked for long life, but have asked for wisdom and knowledge for yourself that you may govern my people over whom I have made you king, wisdom and knowledge are granted to you. I will also give you riches, possessions, and honor, such as none of the kings had who were before you, and none after you shall have the like.

God blessed Solomon with rare prophetic giftings. He brought results to Queen Sheba's complex problems. Solomon was the most efficient Project Manager in his times; he planned the temple project and assigned over 150,000 human resource to the temple's building project. Solomon loved his people such that he made provisions for their time of weakness during the dedication of the temple after completion. He created a pact with God. He said to God; whenever people go out of line and they fall short of God's laws and they look towards the newly built temple, please answer them". God agreed leading to the establishment of this promise found in 2 Chronicles 7:14 - *if my people who are called by my name humble themselves, and pray and seek my face and turn from their wicked ways, then I will hear from heaven and will forgive their sin and heal their land.*

In 20 years, Solomon had accomplished major success; he's completed the temple for God, built cities, ruled wisely and stay rooted in worship. Towards the end of his life, Solomon compromised and bowed to other gods. Solomon was baited with women, and the devil's final plan was to redirect his worship God had warned Israelites against intermarriage with pagan women because they will turn their hearts away after their gods. The consequences of Solomon's departure from the true worship of Yahweh was dire: the kingdom was torn apart amongst others.

Solomon's Foundation

What pushed a king with such past record of love for the Lord to a point of compromising on worship? What drove a king who was granted the privilege of building a house for the God of all gods to go build high places for other gods? How did a king who pleased God and got God to write new laws of forgiveness sponsor the enemies of god? The answer that comes to mind is - *If the foundations are destroyed, What can the righteous do?- Psalm 11:3.*

Unrepaired crooked foundations will destroy the building when erected. When foundational problems are not addressed, the worshipper becomes polluted from the source. *Ecclesiastes 1:15*

What is crooked cannot be made straight and what is lacking cannot be numbered, says Solomon, the Preacher, the King of Israel. Solomon's worship was polluted because he did not resolve the errors and curses in His DNA.

His father David was in the wrong place at the wrong time when He was supposed to be at war. There was the spirit of complacency and negligence at play in the life of David the day he saw Bathsheba taking her bath. His sexual relations with the Uriah's wife may be easily pointed out as the beginning of David's problem with God; David's problems was made possible through complacency and negligence. The process for Israel's king would be similar to this: *In the spring season is when kings go to battle.* Similar events re-occurred in Solomon's time. He neglected an instruction that seemed harmless: *You must not marry them, because they will turn your hearts to their gods - 1 Kings 11:1.*

God is bound by His covenants. There are numerous of them. All of His words are covenants. All His creations, light, darkness, the earth, the heavens are all bound by His covenants. Part of the covenant made with the sun is that; though the sun provide light for us on the earth, it does not mean there are things our eyes will be able to see under the sun. This means, certain things God has concealed from us. Visibility of things do not make them real. The invisibility of things does not make them unreal.

5

ALTAR OF ALTARS

Our first outside worship meeting was at Best Western hotel. The location was secured the last meeting when every other meeting space was booked. The Lord told us that there were people who had already dug the trenches and built Him an altar at the hotel. On getting to the hotel, the hotel manager said the space we've come to rent has inexplicably attracted and hosted new and growing Church gathering. She said many Churches who started here in that banquet hall moved out because the space was no longer sufficient because of Church growth. I smiled when she told me that, because I knew the Lord had told us about some who had built him altars from that Banquet hall. We spent 5 months at the Banquet hall; before we moved out.

When we moved out; we didn't move out because we were out of space, the hotel became too expensive per meeting and we needed a cheaper place. We found an elementary school that housed us and have us use their gym for our gatherings. The Lord approved of the place and told us to get ready to war and dethrone the principality in the area before we could build an altar for Yahweh. By the end of 1 year and 4 months, God's altar was fully established in the region. On the day our assignment was completed in that region, we had no clue it was our last worship there. God spoke and he said, the school will suddenly become known for academic excellence and the children and attending this school will be known as high flyers. Later in the week, the school contacted us about a renovation that was about to begin and we had to move to another location.

The Power on Yahweh's Altar

The worship altar is as powerful as the quality of worship offered on it. Altars are the most powerful and highly-contested-for point of worship. In Church gatherings, if the voice of flesh, voices of people, voice of emotion, voice of bias or any other than the voice of the Holy Spirit ever speaks through the minister from an altar where the presence of God dwells, the altar will spit you out; or the presence of God will depart. In an altar where true worship is offered, the heat of the fire gets hot that darkness cannot come near.

A worship altar of Yahweh that does not lack fire is the most dangerous place for witchcraft and workers of iniquity. In the early days of our ministry, the Lord warned us about a pending demonic intrusion into our worship team but we were bias. The Lord warned us again and again, we didn't listen and the demonic intruder became part of the worship team. Like every bias person, we thought the face and description the Lord showed us didn't match what the Lord had told us. We tuned in the heat of our worship and inquired of the Lord to reveal to us more.

During our 6 hours worship unto the Lord, a woman came to worship with us. She was in town from one of the rural towns. She said she came to worship with us because she needed a place where she could soak into God's presence. She needed to worship the Lord desperately. After worship, she said she had a word to us from the

Lord. She said she was not sure if she should deliver the message. She eventually did. She said there was a demonic agent in our worship team whom the Lord is set to expose in a major way. We knew the Lord sent her from afar as an answered prayer.

Then the Lord showed me in a dream the same individual on our worship team. In the dream, they were absent from the worship sessions and I asked them why they had been absent. The individual said they are deep in witchcraft practice but the fire on the altar of worship is getting too hot for them, hence they can no longer come close to worship by the altar. When I woke up from a dream; it was I could not believe what I had just seen. The same morning was our next worship session. Getting to the Church, one of our prominent worship team mates did not show up. Though I had heard their confession in my dream, I truly wished it was only a dream but it was not. The individual showed up later with a lie and eventually said there are things preventing them from serving on the worship team.

This is one of the deep mysteries of the altar of Yahweh. When an altar is truly of Yahweh, the altar carries live fire. The more worship on the altar, the hotter the fire burns. Agents of darkness in the Churches have one major mission; to quench the fire on the altar. They know if they are successfully in taking out the fire from the altar; the spirit of God departs from that altar. If they are unable to quench the fire; they flee and go to discredit missions.

The God That Answers By Fire

I do not have the entire revelation of altars, but I went back to my bread and found out that it wasn't totally done and was not edible. And thereafter, The Lord said clearly it was a worship unto Him. This brings to mind how en privileged to see to be shown a little bit by the Lord. The Lord spoke to me about his delight in my cooking. And He said He counts that as worship unto Him when I do the things I do joyfully. This opened up my eyes to the subject of worship.

Back in the spring of 2018, I had a strong desire to make our bread. And I purposed in my heart to dedicate the bread to the Lord since it was my debut bread. I kneaded the bread and baked it. When the bread was taken out of the oven, it smelled really nice and looked good. I turned off the oven and set the bread aside. While getting ready to slice the bread; I saw smoke coming out of the oven and as I moved closer to see if the oven was still turned on, it wasn't and the smoke went down gently and was cleared off.

What's an Altar?

An altar is a place of sacrifice. The way altar works is that for every altar built for the worship of Yahweh, there is always a priest. Whenever there is an altar at a location, there must be a priest at the altar in that location. A worshipper can become God's living altar. Hosea 8:11 says "Because Ephraim has made many altaras for sin, They have become for him altars for sinning". God's worshippers are His worshippers. For an altar to be a valid place of worship, there has to be the presence of these three:

1. The Entity
2. The Offeror
3. The Sacrifice

The Entity

The entity is the receiver of the sacrifice. There are two classes of recipients of the sacrifice on the altar. The entity is either the Lord or satan. If you worship before an altar. There is an entity receiving that worship. If it is not Yahweh, then it is the devil. The Entity is the receiver of the sacrifice. There are two classes of recipients of the sacrifice on the altar. The entity is either the Lord God or satan. If you worship before an altar. There is an entity receiving that worship. If it is not Yahweh, then it is the devil.

Yahweh's Altar

Whenever an altar is raised up for the Lord; God's name remain on there forever. When God has been worshipped in a place truthfully, God's presence remains there. Though the presence of God is mobile; but when a person dedicates a place to the Lord, God's presence abides in the place. This is one of the reasons that a spiritually sensitive person can discern a house where abundance of prayers and worship is raised up unto the Lord.

Yahweh's Altar on The Street

We were taking an evening walk in the summer of 2018. As we passed by a neighborhood; the Lord said to us, "you see that house, there is a fellowship of God's people in there". It was highly unlikely in our neighbourhood because most of the people we had invited to fellowship were not believers. We continued with our walk. About 1 hour and 45 minutes later, we were returning and an older lady had stepped out of the house; she said hello to us as we passed. I told my husband I needed to speak to the lady; as I went to speak to her, it turned out that she was a non-English speaker and was speaking Spanish on the phone. Her daughter came out to speak with me and she spoke English. I asked her, Is there a fellowship gathering here? I continued and said to her, we're believers and the Lord said to us that there's a gathering of His children here tonight. She looked at me surprisingly and said yes. She said her parents are Pastors visiting from Puerto Rico for their grandchild's birthday and it's turned into a prayer session. I called my husband to come and hear what's going on. Apparently, the Lord was saying to us that there had been a worship altar raised up for Him here. We were invited to come in to fellowship with them; when we got there - only about 4 people spoke English, the rest spoke Spanish. One person became our translator, we taught them simple yoruba worship songs and we all began to worship. The spirit of God flowed heavily. This is one of the mysteries of the altar of God. The Holy Spirit upon the altar of God speaks.

Satanic Altars on The Street

If believers are afraid to bring God's altar into the streets, the devil is not. Satanic agents are used in many dark places to set up satan's altar on roadsides, in streets, 4-way stops, 3-way stops and at other places of interests. Many times on the road side while growing up in Nigeria, I lost count of the numbers of freshly served egg and red oil used for sacrifice laid bare on the road early in the morning on my way to school. There are similar sights in see are satanic altars on the road in some Asian countries and in the US. These sacrifices are everywhere. For a sacrifice to be laid down at any location, there are altars.

Many of the road accidents, blood shed of animals and humans on the highways are not a form of sacrifice. During many festive seasons, many satanic sacrifices take place in specific places, the devil uses open altars on the road as a source of blood collection and that's why some road accidents occur, resulting in blood bath. Abortion clinics also fall into this category.

Where the worshippers of the Living God abound, these street altars vanishes and the shedding of blood comes to a stop. This is one of the reasons the power of God is made sufficient to the worshipper. The worshipper of Yahweh is a living sacrifice, and in the worshipper is God's living altar. The purity levels of the sacrifice determines the temperature of the altar. The temperature of the altar determines whether impurities can come near the altar or not. Usually altars with extreme temperatures are a no-go zone for satanic agents, and vice versa, lukewarm altars are a breeding ground for satanic pollutions.

How The Devil Perverts Altars

It is spiritually costly to build an altar. Whether you decide to erect an altar for the Lord within your house or you decide to consecrate a place of worship to the Lord. The spiritual cost is very high. This is the reason why witchcraft through the spirit of Jezebel seeks to pull down altars.

For every altar assigned to worship God. There is always a priest. When they say the altar at a location, there is always a priest identified with that altar.. If there is an altar, without a priest, the altar is as invalid. There are no 2 high priests, but only one for every of Yahweh's altar. The priest is responsible for the spiritual state of the altar, ensuring the fire of God never runs out, and constant undiluted worship is offered to the Lord. To pervert an altar, the devil is looking for ways to detract the priest of the Lord who carries the Holy oil and the authority of God. The devil seeks all avenues to get access to the priest for the purpose of corruption.

For the work of perversion and corruption, the spirit of Jezebel and the spirit of witchcraft works in collaboration . comes into play. The spirit of witchcraft seeks to bring under its subjection priests while the spirit of Jezebel seeks to gather prophets together. Ahab as the priest of the land had the authority to relate with the prophets. Through the influence of Ahab, Jezebel had access to the prophets. She congregated the prophets under her. Any prophet that submits themselves to Ahab becomes a servant of Jezebel. They are under jezebel's patrol including their altars. The day Jezebel takes hold of any altar, the spirit of God departs. Once the spirit of witchcraft and Jezebel locates Yahweh's altar; these spirits have one goal, to subdue the priest, throw them out of Yahweh's presence and desecrate the altar.

Perversion of Family Altars (I)

There are a lot of ministers of God whose anointing has been polluted by witchcraft and has been thrown out of God's presence - with the spirit of Jezebel and witchcraft dealing with them from within their spouse.

A worshipper looking to get married needs to go on an extended worship-prayer retreat to ask the Lord to open up their spiritual eyes concerning their bride-to-be or groom-to-be. A lot of worshippers have been caught in the nest of witchcraft in the place of marriage while making a choice of spouse.

When revival wants to enter into a nation, it begins with one person. If the person is married, the revival spreads into the immediate family; and from the immediate family, the fire spreads into the community and many cities catch fire. Witchcraft agents are not sent out to go after ordinary people - "For she has cast down many wounded, And all who were slain by her were strong men" -

Proverbs 7:26. Witchcraft agents go after mighty men and women of God to hinder them from building worship altars for Yahweh.

The Lord brought our way a minister of God who was in deep trouble. We had been praying and God decided to open up His revelation unto us. God began by saying "A salt has lost its taste, the salt is complaining that they are trampling on it. That is what happens when a man decides to go and marry from the kingdom of darkness. The Lord said, this person was anointed with his oil, but he rejected the oil, laid down the oil to conform with the standards of the world. The Lord said, the minister chose his wife over His holy oil, and he ended up marrying a witch". When we shared the prophecy with the minister. He said that was true. He said he chose his wife over the anointing of God over His life. He says the wife does not like the church they used to go where he was a minister; and he left in order to please her. He said it had gotten so bad that his wife threatens to divorce him because she thinks "he's too spiritual". As he was being ministered to that moment; the Lord said to tell him, "don't think your wife do not know you're praying for the deliverance of your family". As soon as we finished ministering to him; his wife called him, asking to report his husband saying, 'why is her praying? What is her husband praying for? The husband is too spiritual. The husband spends more time praying instead of spending time with the family". The wife will jump out of the car whenever the couple is driving when the song in the background is an anointed worship music. When the husband plans to attend a prayer retreat or a 3-day extended fast, she goes to book a compulsory family vacation dragging the husband along, ensuring he misses his prayer retreat. The husband decides to rise up to pray at midnight, the wife complains she feels abandoned, and the husband asked if it is okay to move his prayer time to another time. The situation here is that of bewitchment to prevent him from building an altar for Yahweh or ever walking in the glory of his anointing.

In this situation; there's an active witchcraft spirit at work; whose assignment is to deter the man's service to God and purposefully prevents him from raising up an altar to God. The simple truth is that many men and women whom God's anointed design is upon their lives have been wrongfully married to high-ranking agents of darkness who will lose the gates of hell the moment their spouse attempts to enter into the worship of Yahweh.

Perversion of Family Altars (II)

Another way the devil perverts family altars is the use of one spouse unknowingly to deter the other spouse from raising altars to the Lord. In some situations, the men who are supposed to be the priest of the home are not walking in that office. Hence the woman takes over as the spiritual leader of the family. The husband seeing the wife's commitment begins to mock the wife's spirituality, saying 'she's becoming a weird fanatic". It takes a deeper type of God's grace for such spouse to stay stronger in their walk with God.

SECTION TWO

AN EXPLORATION INTO THE HEART OF VIRTUOUS WORSHIPPERS

6

ABEL

The men of old were mastercrafters and arrangers of worship. With the Holy Spirit and specificity, they demolished every other altars that exalted itself against Yahweh, they turned to null and void the altars of Yahweh's enemies and they built Yahweh's altar; one that swallows every other altar. Worship was the sword they wielded and praise was their sheath. The weight of national intercession never weighed they down; they were indeed true friends of Yahweh. Every altar built by these worshippers atoned for the sins of others and saved others of national disaster.

In addition to righteousness imputed unto faithful builders of worship altars are also great returns on investment of their sacrifices. The works of these great worshippers have preserved the destiny of man and has brought blessings to humanity.

Abel

The Earliest Worshipper With the Prophecy of the First Fruit and Lamb Offering

Abel, the second child of Adam and Eve was one of the earliest human worshippers in the scriptures. His parents, Adam and Eve, were the first group of worshippers, but they fell on their mission to continue to worship and honor the Lord when they submitted to the serpent. Then comes their son Abel who worshipped the Lord.

Though he was murdered for worshipping the Lord, Abel's worship was never a one-off worship, it was a worship that revealed the plans of God to mankind.

Genesis 4:3-7 NLT

When it was time for some harvest, Cain presented some of his crops as a gift to the Lord. Abel; also brought a gift - the best portions of the firstborn lambs from his flock. The Lord accepted Abel and his gift, but he did not accept CAin and his gift. This made Cain very angry, and he looked dejected. "Why are you so angry?" the Lord asked Cain. "Why do you look so dejected? You will be accepted if you do what is right. But if you refuse to do what is right, then watch out! Sin is crouching at the door, eager to control you. But you must subdue it and be its master." One day Cain suggested to his brother, "Let's go out into the fields." And while they were in the field, Cain attacked his brother, Abel, and killed him.

Abel was blessed with prophetic insight. He discerned the heart of God and knew the kind of offering that would please the Lord. Abel was one prophet who never uttered a word of prophecy or named the altar he raised up to God but he prophesied about his offering during his worship. In worship, Abel prophesied about two major types of offerings: *The Lamb Offering and The First Fruit offerings.* Prophet Abel, a man had the earliest revelations of honoring the Lord with the first of his produce. A man who was already working in the revelation of first fruits offering that would be given to Moses who did not belong to his generation. Abel caught the revelation given to Moses and written in Exodus 23:19a: *"You shall* bring the choice first fruits of your soil into the house of the LORD your God".

The second aspect of Abel's prophetic worship is in his choice of animal. He offered firstborn lambs from his flocks. Giving way to the Passover offering which the Lord commanded Moses to institute during Israel's slavery in Egypt several generations after the passing of Abel.

Exodus 21:28 NKJV

Then Moses called for all the elders of Israel and said to them, "Pick out and take lambs for yourselves according to your families, and kill the Passover lamb. And you shall take a bunch of hyssop, dip it in the blood that is in the basin, and strike the lintel and the two doorposts with the blood that is in the basin. And none of you shall go out of the door of his house until morning. For the Lord will pass through to strike the Egyptians; and when He sees the blood on the lintel and on the two doorposts, the Lord will pass over the door and not allow the destroyer to come into your houses to strike you. And you shall observe this thing as an ordinance for you and your sons forever. It will come to pass when you come to the land which the Lord will give you, just as He promised, that you shall keep this service. And it shall be, when your children say to you, 'What do you mean by this service?' that you shall say, 'It is the Passover sacrifice of the Lord, who passed over the houses of the children of Israel in Egypt when He struck the Egyptians and delivered our households.' " So the people bowed their heads and worshiped. Then the children of Israel went away and did so; just as the Lord had commanded Moses and Aaron, so they did.

Abel's passover prophecy was also split into two timelines:

Timeline of the Law: the Passover Lamb & Burnt Offering *Before Jesus:* The blood of the Passover Lamb offerings was spilled as a replacement for the lives of the firstborns of Israel that would have been lost when the angels of destruction visited Egypt. The lamb, which is a young ram is also of great significance and only one of the few animals permissible for burnt offerings in the atonement of sins.

Post-Timeline of the Law, Jesus our Passover Lamb
Jesus, the Lamb of God was the fulfillment of the 2nd tier of Abel's prophetic worship after the timeline of the law. *John was noted to have revealed the identity of Jesus to his disciples when he sighted Jesus. He said, "Behold, the Lamb of God, who takes away the sin of the world! - John 1:29.* Apostle Paul addressed the church at Corinth: *Therefore purge out the old leaven, that you may be a new lump, since you truly are unleavened. For indeed Christ, our Passover, was sacrificed for us.- 1 Corinthians 5:7.*

Although he never named the offering he gave unto the Lord, Abel's altar unto the Lord was the altar of the first fruits and of the lamb offering. Abel worshipped the Lord with best *portions of the firstborn lambs* from his flock giving us a clue of what was to come and what kind of offering the Lord accepted from the Israelites as well as the offering of His only son - the firstborn of the dead..

Why was Abel's worship chosen?
We may never get the full revelation of why Abel's offering was accepted over His brother. However we were told *Cain presented* some of his crops as a gift to the Lord. Abel; also brought a gift - the best portions of the firstborn *lamb.*

The mystery for the acceptance of *offering of the First born and the best portions of his animals.*

Abel's was in a place of spiritual rot. God gave Him a reason: *If you do well, will you not be accepted? And if you do not do well sin lies at the door. And its desire is for you, but you should rule over it.* - Genesis 4:7. A quality spiritual life is important to offering acceptable worship to the Lord God.

7

JOB

GOD BOASTS WITH JOB

Then the Lord said to Satan, "have you considered my servant Job? There is no one on earth like him; he is blameless and upright, a man who fears God and shuns evil

JOB 1:8

Job is often remembered for the calamities that befell him. He was extremely wealthy; spiritually, mentally and in material. Not many realize that Job was a worshipper. Job was a minstrel, he worshipped God on his harp and his flute. When disaster came upon him, he could no longer play his harp and flute as he used to. In place of worship, when his afflicted soul played, his harp brought forth mourning and the sound of his flute was as the voice of cry. Like Job, it is certain that all worshippers will go through their times of test. A time when there will be afflictions, despite living in righteously before the Lord. The worshipper is guaranteed victory at the end.

Here are some truths that every worshipper must know; The worshipper wins the Father's love heart, the worshipper delights the Father more, the worshipper gets more attention from the Father, the worshipper receives more favor from the Father, the worshipper receives more blessing and the worshipper is tried and tested harder than the non-worshipper.

The Battle of Worship

When the time came for Job to fight in the war of the worshipper. It came unusually. Job got into the fight because his worship pleased so much that the Lord showed off Job to satan, but satan accused Job of receiving God's blessing, hence all the worship. In other words, Satan said to God, let me help you shake and sift him, and see if he won't renounce you. With this request, God gives satan permission to test Job.

There comes a time when satan goes before the Lord to ask to accuse the righteous and help test them. Many times, the Lord gives permission but maintains authority over the very life of the righteous. There is no one whom the enemy sifts that stays except those whom the Lord Jesus Himself intercedes for.

Despite his dilapidated health, death of his family, loss of wealth, Job refused to curse God. He refused to deny God. This too, is worship.

During the battle of worship, the worshipper should not find it surprising that it is usually a lone war, because the world never loves in affliction. Job was blessed to have friends who showed up in his affliction. These friends knew the word of God, but they had no revelation into what God was doing with Job. They knew so well the justice side of God and they were almost sure that Job wronged God. This passive accusation, was from the devil.

Reflecting on the Worship Lifestyle

Like any worshipper in affliction would do, Job reflects on his lifestyle, and found no blemish but pure worship. He calls God to examine him more to check for any flaw in his lifestyle.. He focuses on six major ares, asking for the examination of God, knowing he had fully given his all to God.

Family Worship: The fear of God was found in Job, like everyone other worshipper. Job feared God so much that he would sacrifice burnt offerings on behalf of each of his children, just incase they had sinned against God. He brought his family before the Lord constantly.(Job 1:4-5)

Righteousness: He worked righteously such that falsehood and deceit were not found in him. His focus was on God and he never wandered away. Job 31:5-9

Discipline : Made a covenant with his eyes and was very disciplined with women. *"If my heart has been enticed by a woman or if I have lurked at my neighbor's door"* - Job 31:9. Job refused to go the way of the wayward. He stayed away from things that could easily beset him and throw him out of God's presence.

Giving: Catered for the poor, the widow, the fatherless. He thought about others too. Job availed his resources to the hungry, and all who were in need. This, to him was worship too

Material: Job realized he could not worship his possessions and still worship the Living God. He never made any of his fine jewelry or materials his hope or god (Job 31:24). This was part one of the several ways why God found him righteous.

Love: Worshipped with love and in love. There was so much love found in the life of Job that he would not rejoice when his enemies fell or were consumed - (Job 31:29). One of the quickest ways a worshipper could lose touch with God is rejoicing at the fall of a foe. God by nature never wants any of his children to get destroyed. However, the justice side of God has to come into effect when people refuse to accept his love, grace and mercy but continue in wickedness.

Having lived in righteousness, Job had no clue what he had done wrong that he challenged God. *"What have I done to you, O water of men? Why have you set me as your target so that I am a burden to myself? - Job 7:20.*

Revelations of Job

In Job's affliction, Job had a lot of questions he asked God, he uttered a lot of statements. God had gone quiet. After a while, God responded, giving Job many revelations of Himself and His works. here are some of the revelations Job received.

#1 **Construction the earth:** In creating the earth, God had it well planned. He took the measurements of the earth, before the foundations were made. And when the foundations were made, he fastened the foundations to some holder, maybe a line. (Job 38:4-5). This revelation expands on what God told Moses about how He had created the earth with his word. It revealed the processes God took.

#2 **Creation of the clouds:** God also told Job about the making of the clouds; He told Job that the cloud wears a garment, and is wrapped in swaddling band, having a limit and doors, giving insight as to why the cloud hasn't fallen over the earth.(Job 38:9)

#3 **Sea:** God opened up the secrets of the sea too. The reason why the sea had not left its place to get onto the land was given. God said the sea is being shut with doors so that it never goes beyond its place (Job 38:8)

#4 **Death:** While Job's friends were not given the revelation: He was given revelation into the entrance place of death and told that the place is guarded by gates.

#5 **Light:** God began to ask Job questions about Job's understanding the distribution of light of light (Job 38:24). I doubt if Job knew anything as such existed, but Job had something new to think about.

#6 **Snow & Hail :** God told Job about a storehouse of snow and hail. The place where snow and hail are stored until released to the earth, these elements the Lord reserves for day of war and trouble.(Job 38:22)

All of these revelations of God are available to those who worship God diligently and faithfully. Job's story teaches that the worshipper is not omitted from trials and tests, but through it all the attitude of the worshipper matters.

Jacob

Worshipper, Father of the 12 Tribes of Israel

Instituted:

Altar at Bethel

Tithing

Mahanaim

Peniel

8

JACOB

JACOB RENAMED ISRAEL

> So He said to him, "What is your name? He said, "Jacob."
> And He said, "Your name shall no longer be called Jacob, but
> Israel; for you have struggled with God and with men, and
> have prevailed."

GENESIS 32: 3:13

Jacob was a worshipper who still had deception buried deep
in his life. This deception held him down even as a worshipper. In
every instance in his life, he would see the hand and move of God, but
was not able to proceed into his destiny as a new nation because
there was a stronghold of deception in his roots.

Deception 1:

Genesis 25:29-34

*Now Jacob cooked a stew; and Esau came in from the field, and he was
weary. And Esau said to Jacob, "Please feed me with that same red stew, for
I am weary." Therefore his name was called Edom. But Jacob said, "Sell me
your birthright as of this day." And Esau said, "Look, I am about to die; so
what is this birthright to me?"Then Jacob said, "Swear to me as of this day."*

So he swore to him, and sold his birthright to Jacob. And Jacob gave Esau bread and stew of lentils; then he ate and drank, arose, and went his way. Thus Esau despised his birthright.

Deception 2:

Genesis 27:18-36 (NKJV)

So he went to his father and said, "My father."And he said, "Here I am. Who are you, my son?" Jacob said to his father, "I am Esau your firstborn; I have done just as you told me; please arise, sit and eat of my game, that your soul may bless me." But Isaac said to his son, "How is it that you have found it so quickly, my son?" And he said, "Because the Lord your God brought it to me." Isaac said to Jacob, "Please come near, that I may feel you, my son, whether you are really my son Esau or not." So Jacob went near to Isaac his father, and he felt him and said, "The voice is Jacob's voice, but the hands are the hands of Esau." And he did not recognize him, because his hands were hairy like his brother Esau's hands; so he blessed him. Then he said, "Are you really my son Esau?" He said, "I am He said, "Bring it near to me, and I will eat of my son's game, so that my soul may bless you." So he brought it near to him, and he ate; and he brought him wine, and he drank. Then his father Isaac said to him, "Come near now and kiss me, my son." And he came near and kissed him; and he smelled the smell of his clothing, and blessed him and said: "Surely, the smell of my son Is like the smell of a field Which the Lord has blessed. Therefore may God give you

Of the dew of heaven, Of the fatness of the earth, And plenty of grain and wine. Let peoples serve you, And nations bow down to you. Be master over your brethren, And let your mother's sons bow down to you. Cursed be everyone who curses you, And blessed be those who bless you! Now it happened, as soon as Isaac had finished blessing Jacob, and Jacob had scarcely gone out from the presence of Isaac his father, that Esau his brother came in from his hunting. He also had made savory food, and brought it to his father, and said to his father, "Let my father arise and eat of his son's game, that your soul may bless me." And his father Isaac said to him, "Who are you?" So he said, "I am your son, your firstborn, Esau." Then Isaac trembled exceedingly, and said, "Who? Where is the one who hunted game and brought it to me? I ate all of it before you came, and I have blessed him—and indeed he shall be blessed." When Esau heard the words of his father, he cried with an exceedingly great and bitter cry, and said to his father, "Bless me— me also, O my father!" But he said, "Your brother came with deceit and has taken away your blessing." And Esau said, "Is he not rightly named Jacob? For he has supplanted me these two times. He took away my birthright, and now look, he has taken away my blessing".

These major deceptive acts of Jacob became a curse and a hindrance into God's plan for Jacob. Jacob fled from his brother and left home. Shortly after he fled, he had an encounter with God, the encounter at Bethel.

The Altar at Bethel

Jacob had the strange encounter into a heavenly portal on his way to

Haran where he met with God. God established a covenant with him and he worshipped the Lord, setting up an altar unto the Lord, and giving the altar the name - Bethel.

Genesis 28:10-12

"Now Jacob left Beersheba and went towards Haran. So he came to a certain place and stayed there all night, because the sun had set. And he took one of the stones of that place and put it at his head, and he lay down in that place to sleep. Then he dreamed, and behold, a ladder was set up on the earth, and its top reached to heaven; and there the angels of God were ascending and descending on it. And behold, the Lord stood above it and said: "I am the Lord God of Abraham your father and the God of Isaac; the land on which you lie I will give to you and your descendants. Also your descendants shall be as the dust of the earth; you shall spread abroad to the west and the east, to the north and the south; and in you and in your seed all the families of the earth shall be blessed. Behold, I am with you and will keep you wherever you go, and will bring you back to this land; for I will not leave you until I have done what I have spoken to you." Then Jacob awoke from his sleep and said, "Surely the Lord is in this place, and I did not know it." And he was afraid and said, "How awesome is this place! This is none other than the house of God, and this is the gate of heaven!" Then Jacob rose early in the morning, and took the stone that he had put at his head, set it up as a pillar, and poured oil on top of it. And he called the name of that place Bethel; but the name of that city had been Luz previously. Then Jacob made a vow, saying, "If God will be with me, and keep me in this way that I am going, and give me bread to eat and clothing to put on, so that I come back to my father's house in peace, then the Lord shall be my God. And this stone which I have set as a pillar shall be God's house, and of all that You give me I will surely give a tenth to You."

Jacob had worship in his heart, though he had deception his life. The deceiver in him had just stolen the blessing of his brother. His brother's virtue had been handed over to him, his brother's place in leadership was now his, his older brother will never become superior to Jacob in leadership. It doesn't stop at that, the descendants of his brother Esau, would also bow to Jacob's descendants according to the last blessings released by their father. When Jacob encountered the Lord at Bethel, God confirms the blessing to Jacob, promising generational blessings to Jacob. Jacob responded with worship. He built an altar for the Lord, poured oil upon the Lord and placed the name of God upon the place, calling it - Beth-El, meaning *"House of El"* or *"House of God"*. He further prays to God for protection and promises to give back to God 1/10th of all his net worth. Whenever the name of God is placed upon a place or a thing, the presence of God never departs. Many times today, many people still have encounters with roots of deception still present in their own lives.

Three Covenants At Bethel

1. Worship of God
2. Bethel as a House of God
3. The covenant of one-tenth.

Many times when praying along with people; God has revealed that He has great plans for people, but there is still some deception present. Getting into a place of revelation means that God to draw people closer to Him. He wants to show them what He has planned, but moving into the realm of living in His plan is entirely a different thing and requires more than revelation.

The next phase of Jacob's life was at his Uncle's, Laban. He worked for Laban in exchange of 7 years of work to marry Rachel. Jacob got to work immediately, and by the end of 7 years, he was ready to marry Rachel whom he loved.

Genesis 29:19-25 (NKJV)

And Laban said, "It is better that I give her to you than that I should give her to another man. Stay with me." So Jacob served seven years for Rachel, and they seemed only a few days to him because of the love he had for her. Then Jacob said to Laban, "Give me my wife, for my days are fulfilled, that I may go in to her." And Laban gathered together all the men of the place and made a feast. Now it came to pass in the evening, that he took Leah his daughter and brought her to Jacob; and he went in to her. And Laban gave his maid Zilpah to his daughter Leah as a maid. So it came to pass in the morning, that behold, it was Leah. And he said to Laban, "What is this you have done to me? Was it not for Rachel that I served you? Why then have you deceived me?

The root of deception in Jacob's life was unresolved, and brought deception upon his destiny too. He had just served 7 years only to be deceived into marrying Leah, a woman that he never loved or planned to marry. However, inside of Jacob's heart was deep affection for Rachel, the one whom he loves and he didn't mind paying his uncle another 7 years of hard work just too marry Rachael. Jacob's life was at his Uncle's, Laban. He worked for Laban in exchange of 7 years of work to marry Rachel. Jacob got to work immediately, and by the end of 7 years, he was ready to marry Rachel whom he loved. Rachel was given to him. From his marriage were 12 children which became the tribe of Israel.

The deception still present in the life of Jacob left significant footprints in the future nation that the Lord was set to begin, even before the seeds that would make up the new nation was formed. Many who have been marked for God's worship are usually great targets of satan who attempts to ruin the worship future of the worshipper before the worshipper ever gets to know about the oil of worship upon them. Jacob found himself in a marriage with two women who were two sisters. One he loved, one he didn't. With his

God being a righteous God, the one who defends the defenseless, and the voice of the oppressed - God chose to open up the womb of the unloved wife, Leah and close up the womb of Racheal, Jacob's loved wife. Leah's loveless marriage was of great pain and each time she gave birth to a child, she would name the child a name reflecting the circumstances of her marriage and the state of her heart, thereby prophesying the future of her children, decreeing the destiny of tribes within an entire nation. With Rachael, the loved wife of Jacob, there was the pain of barrenness, shame and jealousy within her until she eventually birthed Joseph.

Children of Jacob: The Tribe of Israel			
Position	*Names*	*Meaning of Names*	*Mother*
1st	Reuben	Affliction	**Leah**
2nd	Simeon	Unloved	**Leah**
3rd	Levi	Attachment	**Leah**
4th	Judah	Praise	**Leah**
5th	Dan	Judgement	**Bilhah, Rachel's Maid**
6th	Naphtali	Wrestle	**Bilhah, Rachel's Maid**
7th	Gad	Troop	**Zilpah, Leah's Maid**
8th	Asher	Happy	**Zilpah, Leah's Maid**
9th	Issachar	Wages	**Leah**
10th	Zebulun	Endowment	**Leah**
11th	Dinah	Controversy	**Leah**
12th	Joseph	Additional Son	**Racheal**

13th	Benjamin	Right Hand	**Rachael**

The Invite To Bethel

Though Jacob's work prospered at Laban's, but his life had been bounded in unsettleness, slavery, and failure to keep up with peace in marriage. Laban continually deceived him despite his hard work. After 20 years, Jacob's worship on the way to Haran at Laban's house rose up as a memorial to the Lord and God said to Jacob;

Genesis 31:11-13 (NKJV)

Then the Angel of God spoke to me in a dream, saying, 'Jacob.' And I said, 'Here I am.' And He said, 'Lift your eyes now and see, all the rams which leap on the flocks are streaked, speckled, and gray-spotted; for I have seen all that Laban is doing to you. I am the God of Bethel, where you anointed the pillar and where you made a vow to Me. Now arise, get out of this land, and return to the land of your family.' "

Though with Jacob's worship and the altar he built at Bethel, God came back to introduce Him as the God of that location; reminding Jacob of the conversation they both had 20 years ago and assuring him that the covenant from that conversation still holds. However; his current life in slavery, oppression under his uncle and family situation no longer looked blurry. God called Jacob out of oppression that night, and said it was time to return back to his family.

Deliverance Precedes Deeper Worship

20 years ago, Jacob travelled alone to Haran through a place Luz which he renamed Bethel after the encounter with God. He set out with his family back home. Jacob knew his trip back home would not be an ordinary encounter. He soon had his first angelic encounter

- which he called the place Mahanaim. From Jacob's life, he had bursts of encounters with God while he had not gotten into what God has called him out for.

Though 20 years had passed that he deceived his brother; there was a curse following him everywhere he went - one that would not be broken until he was delivered. Every worshipper needs deliverance if they have not sought deliverance from curses, strongholds and yokes in their foundation. Without deliverance, worship is short-lived, because the curses and yokes will show up quite often preventing the worshipper from getting deeper into worship with their whole heart.. Deliverance is setting free from anything holding anyone captive. In Jacob's case, he could not move to the next stage of his life because he had lived his life in deceit. He needed deliverance from his foundation of deceit.

God had a plan for him, God wanted to meet him at Bethel - the place of their original covenant, however, he could not carry the deceit still in him into the Holy Place of God at Bethel, though he was the one who set up the altar years ago. God is just and holy - anyone short of holiness cannot come into his presence, hence Jacob's deliverance was had to happen at a location before Bethel and at a time before he got to Bethel. Like Jacob's situation, deliverance is sometimes location sensitive - such that deliverance is tied to a specific location.

Stages of Jacob's Deliverance

Jacbo's deliverance from the time he fled from Esau to the time he returned was progressive and topical. The deliverance of Jacob was not a one-time encounter, it was progressive.

1)   Deliverance From Spiritual Blindness

On the first phase of the journey to his Uncle's house, he met with God and his eyes were opened. He became a seer, and was shown the presence of angelic activities at Bethel. He raise and altar and named the place of his divine encounter. The deliverance of Jacob was not a one-time encounter, it was progressive. Even after God had opened his eyes, his uncle Laban still cheated him, indicating there was an area of his life that still needed deliverance.

2) Deliverance From The Lingering Curse of Deception

Looking back at his experience in the past 20 years, if Jacob could go back in time, he probably would not deceive his brother. On his way back home he prepares to meet with his brother, and to apologize in humility. He would not have done all he did but there was a curse awaiting Jacob from the name he was given birth. His parents found that Jacob had been fighting his brother from the womb, he had held the heels of his brother when they were born His parents gave him the name *"Jacob"* which means *"supplanter"*. Supplanter means one who steals the place of others. Hence, this curse was at work in the life of Jacob and it was also working against him from the external.

20 years after his Bethel encounter, on his way home, Jacob had a man-to-man wrestling encounter with God. To break the curse upon him, a deliverance was needed. God had to take him through the pain of holding forth his brother's heel in the womb, God touched the socket of Jacob's hip (*Genesis 32:25*) to take him back to the moment of his failure and supplanting in order to heal him. It wasn't a gentle fight, it wasn't a fight that lasted 1 hour or 2, it was an all-night warring. Though God came down as man but had to use divine abilities to conquer Jacob, by dislocating his thigh. In seeking deliverance, the worshipper must have the tenacity to fight to the end. *And God who came as Man said, "let me go, for the day breaks". But he said, "I will not let you go unless you bless me!". So He said to him, "What is your name?" He said, "Jacob". And He said, "Your name shall no longer be called Jacob, but Israel, for you have struggled with God and with men, and*

have prevailed". - *Genesis 32:26-28.* Right there, after the encounter, Israel called the name of the place Peniel translated into " *I have seen God face to face".* This kind of deliverance is the deliverance for destiny from foundational troubles. It is required for everyone who intends to get far in worship. It is not a surface deliverance; it is not the kind of deliverance to cast out demons of deception, the spirit of lying or anger; it is the kind of deliverance to uproot foundational roots showing up its symptoms in different forms. These kind of deliverance needs to target the origin of problems in the life of the worshipper like the ancestry, names, problems from the time in the womb, problems inherited through marriage, affliction through territory and many others - these deliverance is thoroughly addressed in our previously published book: Uncursed at Uncursed.Org. The verdict and report of God concerning Jacob was that Jacob prevailed against God, and God changed his name that he became the prince of God. This revelation was what Jacob had that after his last son was born by Rachel who was dying and was named Ben Omi "Son of my sorrows", Jacob changed the name to Benjamin - knowing the prophetic powers in names.

There are many whom the Lord has designed for his worship, but they still have names tying them down into a curse or a demonic cause, they will never be able to fully get into what God has for them. There are many worshippers today who are in a close relationship with sins that are holding them captive. If a thousand truths from the Word of God is spoken to them. Many worshippers truly encounter God when they worship, but there are still remnants of baggage from the past, while some are still covering up their sins. There are many worshippers who hear the sermon warning them against adultery, lies, sexual perversion, yet they will not listen or repent. Many of these people who fall into these categories go on in their journey only to get to a major height and fall a great fall.

Until a worshipper dwells deeply with God, renouncing the ways of old, saying, inviting God into their foundation and saying, *"Here I am Lord, meet with me with your deliverance,"* only then will God come in to ask questions like, "What is your name"? The worshipper's response will determine the course of their life from that moment onwards. Anyone who is drawn into worship must painstakingly revisit their foundations and cut away from what will stop them or cut them away from worship at any point in their journey with God. No woorshipper will hold on to the demonic name, cause, association and go far with God.

The Covenants at Bethel

God's name is powerful; when a worshipper decides to name a place, a thing, or themselves by the name of God, God's presence comes upon the object that has been called by His name. Here are some of the attributes of God at Bethel. These attributes will give you insights into the nature of covenants between Jacob and God at Bethel:

1) **An Everlasting God:** All of God's covenants are eternal and cannot be altered by any generation. He is the God that never changes. He is a keeper of covenants for all generations.

2) **A Faithful God:** He is the God who does not alter the terms of His covenants just because the father has passed away. He is the God that still decrees the articles of the covenants to the children even long after the passing of the parents whom He established the covenant with.

The Covenant of God's House: Jacob said to God at Bethel, *Then Jacob made a vow, saying, "If God will be with me, and keep me in this way that I am going, and give me bread to eat and clothing to put on, so that I come back to my father's house in peace, then the Lord shall be my God. And this stone which I have set as a pillar shall be God's house, and of all that You give me I will surely give a tenth to You.* - Genesis 28:20-22. Jacob set up a pillar and covenanted that the place for God's dwelling. Ever since that day, God's presence overshadowed that location and the place became a house of God. Bethel became full of God's power so much that it became a base for prophets of God, a place where Elijah and Elisha visited, ad where the sons of the prophets - people who had high spiritual authorities dwelled. This, began with Jacob's worship.

The Covenant of Tithing: Jacob promised God at Bethel on his way to his Uncle before he had his family: *If God will be with me, and keep me in this way that I am going, and give me bread to eat and clothing to put on, so that I come back to my father's house in peace, then the Lord shall be my God. And this stone which I have set as a pillar shall be God's house, and of all that You give me I will surely give a tenth to You." - Genesis 28:12.* Long after Jacob was gone; the validity of the covenant remained intact, up until this moment. The Lord referenced this covenant and specifically identified which of their fathers who made this covenant in Malachi 3:6 saying :

> *"For I am the Lord, I do not change; Therefore you are not consumed, O sons of Jacob. Yet from the days of your fathers You have gone away from My ordinances And have not kept them. Return to Me, and I will return to you," Says the Lord of hosts. "But you said, 'In what way shall we return?' "Will a man rob God? Yet you have robbed Me! But you say, 'In what way have we robbed You?' In tithes and offerings. You are cursed with a curse, For you have robbed Me, Even this whole nation. Bring all the tithes into the storehouse, That there may be food in My house, And try Me now in this," Says the Lord of hosts, "If I will not open for you the windows of heaven And pour out for you such blessing That there will not be room enough to receive it. For I am the Lord, I change not; therefore ye sons of Jacob are not consumed.*

The covenant of tithing is tremendously potent in the lives of native and spiritual Israelites. It is one of the covenants remembered when worshippers call God by the name - God of Abraham, Isaac and Jacob. These fathers were worshippers and they were tithers. These fathers placed the name of God upon 1/10th of all their earnings. They consecrated it to God and set it aside for the glory of God. Being a God that never shares his glory with anyone; withholding tithes from the Lord reopens Jacob's pre-deliverance era up. The curse of not paying tithes is as the curse of deception fighting Jacob. He worked hard, yet he labored and was in slavery and the blessing he needed to receive was witheld in heaven. Worship is very costly; one of the ways to find out if we really love God is our willingness and the state of our heart if God is asking us to release back to Him a thing he has blessed us with, and particularly funds.

Brokenness Precedes The Bethel Promises

Going into God's presence in deceit is like wearing a mask. God does not bless a mask. Any worshipper who wants to progress in their worship journey or want to dwell in God's presence perpetually must be delivered completely from curses, yokes and strongholds. An undelivered worshipper is still being held captive, and a prisoner with a tiny window of opportunity to worship God - in a matter of time, their captor grabs them back in chains. Jacob went through a rigorous deliverance encounter before he became Israel. The devil tries to spread the wrong information on deliverance, to keep people away from seeking deliverance. The deliverance of Jacob was in multiple stages and at different times.

Until a believer takes off the mask they wear into the presence of God, until they come to the end of themselves will they meet the blessing of God, it will be a toil and self justification and waste. He was a worshipper and had issues in his own life. Not only encountered the portal of God, but also ran into a company of angels. His life had to do with angelic encounters here on earth. It was important because of the assignment in life, he was supposed to be a nation. As a broken vessel, there was still ies in his life. He had encounters and experiences, yet those things could not bring him to the place of manifestation of the glory. The glories he encountered were transient.

God could have met him for deliverance in Bethel the second time, but it was a place already consecrated to God. After his name had changed and he had met his brother, he was from the curse, his next meeting with God was at Bethel, this time not alone, but with his family. God is the God of covenant and He told Jacob to return back to the place of His covenant with Him. Jacob knew it was not an ordinary meeting. Before Jacob married and had a family, he met with God. Then God invites him back to the place of the covenant after he had a family.

Genesis 35:2-4

Get rid of the foreign gods you have with you, and purify yourselves and change your clothes. Then come, let us go up to Bethel, where I will build an altar to God, who answered me in the day of my distress and who has been with me wherever I have gone." So they gave Jacob all the foreign gods they had and the rings in their ears, and Jacob buried them under the oak at Shechem

Jacob prepared his family to take off all the dirts, idols, filthiness and baggage before they follow him to meet with God. He was probably telling them, you can't go with me to meet the Holy God this way, and he was right. For the family of Jacob, the new Israelites, it was a meeting for generational deliverance. This type of deliverance is still needed today. Some parents were living in sin up until they had their children. A double dose of deliverance is needed. The parents need deliverance, so do the children who were born into iniquity when parents had not met God or have not been delivered from certain curses after they had their children. The children were not born into righteousness and the devil seeks to leverage that A reset is needed and that reset with God's deliverance. This was the encounter with Jacob's family in the presence of God the second time at Bethel.

Genesis 35:6-15

Jacob and all the people with him came to Luz (that is, Bethel) in the land of Canaan. There he built an altar, and he called the place El Bethel, because it was there that God revealed himself to him when he was fleeing from his brother.Now Deborah, Rebekah's nurse, died and was buried under the oak outside Bethel. So it was named Allon Bakuth. After Jacob returned from Paddan Aram, God appeared to him again and blessed him. God said to him, "Your name is Jacob, but you will no longer be called Jacob; your name will be Israel." So he named him Israel. And God said to him, "I am God Almighty; be fruitful and increase in number. A nation and a community of nations will come from you, and kings will be among your descendants. The land I gave to Abraham and Isaac I also give to you, and I will give this land to your descendants after you." Then God went up from himat the place where he had talked with him. Jacob set up a stone pillar at the place where God had talked with him, and he poured a drink offering on it; he also poured oil on it. Jacob called the place where God had talked with him Bethel.

On the family level, breakthrough into worship starts with one willing worshipper, who is willing to sacrifice and pay the price of worship. It was Jacob now Israel in this situation. He paid the price, worship God, fought with God, obtained deliverance and brought his entire family into the presence of God to worship God and obtain the blessing for their descendants.

Joseph

Worshipper and dreamer who feared God

Major Assignments

Delivered an entire nation from famine

Made provision for the entire tribe of Israel in Egypt

9

JOSEPH

JACOB RENAMED ISRAEL

> So He said to him, "What is your name? He said, "Jacob." And He said, "Your name shall no longer be called Jacob, but Israel; for you have struggled with God and with men, and have prevailed."

GENESIS 32: 3:13

Joseph will always be remembered as the worshipper who worshipped the Lord fearfully even if it meant captivity for him. Today, satan is carefully and comfortably seated in the lives of many, deceiving them that the fear of God should be thrown out of the window and because He is the all loving God.

The Fearful God in Worship

The fear of God is a part of the worship of God that is inseparable. There is no worshipper without the fear of God. Jesus pointed to the Lord as the One to be feared. Everyone who goes far into worship reaches a major junction called the intersection of fear. The fear of God grips the worshipper as the presence of the Lord is felt in the moment of worship. In the praises of His people, He is fearful. The coming of the Lord to dwell in worship brings along fear The coming down of the King of kings to the earth comes with a whole lot of power, mountains are melted, anything the Lord meets on the way either flees or is destroyed. The Scripture talks about the reaction of the heaven and earth when they saw the Lord, they fled.

Micah 1:3-4 (BSB)

For behold, the LORD comes forth out of His dwelling place; He will come down and tread on the high places of the earth. The mountains will melt beneath Him, and the valleys will split apart, like wax before the fire, like water cascading down a slope.

This is what it looks like when the Lord comes down. The fear of God is not dispensable in worship. Every worshipper in the Scripture were people who lived life in the fear of God - even Moses. Moses led the Israelites to Sinai, yet he was very fearful at the presence of God.

Hebrews 12:18-21 (NKJV)

For you have not come to the mountain that may be touched and that burned with fire, and to blackness and darkness and tempest, and the sound of a trumpet and the voice of words, so that those who heard it begged that the word should not be spoken to them anymore. (For they could not endure what was commanded: "And if so much as a beast touches the mountain, it shall be stoned or shot with an arrow." And so terrifying was the sight that Moses said, "I am exceedingly afraid and trembling.")

Joseph: A Child Full of Love & of Dreams

Joseph, the first child of Jacob and Rachel. His parents loved each other; his mother Rachel waited for him to arrive and when he finally came, he was indeed a child that the Lord used to bring her healing. Rachel had passed away; the Scripture records, *"Israel loved Joseph more than lad his children, because he was the son of his old age. Also he made him a tunic of many colors"*- Genesis 37:3.

Joseph's life was centered around the theme of garments and dreams. His brothers found that their father loved him, because he got a tunic of many colors. They hated him more when he told his brothers his dreams. Joseph's dreams are highlighted below:

1. **Joseph 1st Dream:** *There we were, binding sheaves in the field. Then behold, my sheaf arose and also stood upright; and indeed your sheaves stood all around and bowed down to my sheaves*

2. **Joseph 2nd Dream:** *"Look, I have dreamed another dream. And this time, the sun, the moon, and the eleven stars bowed down to me."*

Joseph's portion in life had always been laced with envy and jealousy, longer than he had been alive. Joseph's mother Rachel lived in rivalry with her sister Leah, throughout her lifetime in her marriage. Some of the spiritual warfare that faces the worshipper is one that had gone on in the ancestry before they came. Another common war that is found in the life of many worshippers are internal wars - the war from within the household of the worshipper. This is the fulfilment of a prophecy of Jesus in *Mathew 10:36 - A man's enemies will be the members of his own household.'* - The only time a worshipper may be exempted from this prophecy is when the entire household is truly saved, and walking truthfully in the precepts of the Lord, but this is quite rare.

Some of the revelation the Lord has given us in ministry concerning this is very surprising. There are a lot of individuals regardless of how advanced in age they are; or how long they have been in ministry, it is always shocking to know who's been the individual responsible for that affliction. Most of the individuals are masked, and they are very close family members - from under the same roof; sometimes spouse afflicting spouse, parent afflicting child, children afflicting parents. Afflictions from the closest household members are usually the most potent ones. Sometimes the Lord allows the affliction to take place, so he can nurture his worshippers from out of the furnace of affliction. Sometimes God allows the closest people to crush the hearts of the worshipper, so that the worshipper holds no other person high other than Him in their hearts, so the worshipper's all is no longer family, so that the worshipper is no longer intoxicated in the worship of others but the worshipper turns totally to the Only Faithful God.

Genesis 37:23 (NKJV)

So it came to pass, when Joseph had come to his brothers, that they stripped Joseph of his tunic, the tunic of many colors that was on him. Then they took him and cast him into a pit. And the pit was empty; there was no water in it.

Joseph got too that point when his siblings sold him out into slavery because they envied him and wanted to kill his future.

Joseph: The Worshipper's Traits:

Sometimes worshippers stumble into worship in times of oppression. It takes time and encounters for a worshipper to discover their worship assignment, but there are traits that are visible that may be an indication that there's an oil of worship over a life. There are also visible traits that are sometimes present in the lives of those whom God has marked for his worship as found in the Scripture below;

Genesis 39:1-6 (NKJV)

Now Joseph had been taken down to Egypt. And Potiphar, an officer of Pharaoh, captain of the guard, an Egyptian, bought him from the Ishmaelites who had taken him down there. 2 The Lord was with Joseph, and he was a successful man; and he was in the house of his master the Egyptian. 3 And his master saw that the Lord was with him and that the Lord made all he did to prosper in his hand. 4 So Joseph found favor in his sight, and served him. Then he made him overseer of his house, and all that he had he put under his authority. So it was, from the time that he had made him overseer of his house and all that he had, that the Lord blessed the Egyptian's house for Joseph's sake; and the blessing of the Lord was on all that he had in the house and in the field. Thus he left all that he had in Joseph's hand, and he did not know what he had except for the bread which he ate.

Trait #1: Unexplainable Favor of God: Even in affliction, the worshiper is given access to the favor of God. The favor of God was released upon Joseph.

Trait #2: Dedication: Worshipers are given to dedication to their employers. In the workplace, they work diligently. Joseph was highly dedicated

Trait #3: Leadership: Worshipers are good overseers. There is a leadership oil upon them. Joseph was made to lead others

Trait #4: Transference of Blessing: Where there is a worshipper, blessing could be released upon a household, an enterprise or a community. Because of Joseph's presence, his boss was blessed

Joseph: The Worshipper's Dilemma:

The worshipper also gets to a point in their lives where they are faced with hard decisions. Majorly the nature of these choices will be tied to making decisions for God or against God. You may be marked to live your life in the deep worship of God and when the devil sees that, the throws hard choices at you

Genesis 39:6-15 (NKJV)

Now Joseph was handsome in form and appearance And it came to pass after these things that his master's wife cast longing eyes on Joseph, and she said, "Lie with me. "But he refused and said to his master's wife, "Look, my master does not know what is with me in the house, and he has committed all that he has to my hand. There is no one greater in this house than I, nor has he kept back anything from me but you, because you are his wife. How then can I do this great wickedness, and sin against God?" So it was, as she spoke to Joseph day by day, that he did not heed her, to lie with her or to be with her. But it happened about this time, when Joseph went into the house to do his work, and none of the men of the house was inside, that she caught him by his garment, saying, "Lie with me." But he left his garment in her hand, and fled and ran outside. And so it was, when she saw that he had left his garment in her hand and fled outside, hat she called to the men of her house and spoke to them, saying, "See, he has brought in to us a Hebrew to mock us. He came in to me to lie with me, and I cried out with a loud voice. 1And it happened, when he heard that I lifted my voice and cried out, that he left his garment with me, and fled and went outside."

Dilemma #1: Attracting the Satanic Agents: You may attract destiny destroyers because of the colorful destiny in the worship of Yahweh ahead of you. Agents of satan are highly sent after worshippers to pollute with sex, unholy conversations, unprofitable chatter, and every other thing that the Lord hates. Joseph's look got the attention of his master's wife that he asked that he lie with her.

Dilemma #2: Pleasing with a Yes, or Angering with a No : Worshippers are not people-pleasers. A worshipper will get to a broad intersection in life where they will either say "yes" to satisfy others or say "no" to stand for righteousness will get people really angry. Joseph said "no" to his master's wife and she got really angry. Joseph went through this phase, and in his mind, he probably was thinking, how can I do this and lose communion with the Lord. He feared God and the fear of God did not make him think twice about the satanic proposal.

Dilemma #3: Cutting satanic Ties: Worshippers know when to cut satanic relationships. Some relationships are satanically designed. The spirit of accusation is one of the common spirit warring against the worshipper. This was the spirit at work in the life of Portipha's wife. Many spirits will rage and accuse the worshipper false if they do not have their way in the life of a worshipper.

Dilemma #4: Taking God's test in Good Faith: You may have done the right thing and you are still paying the price for doing God. Good may be testing you. In your test, He will never forsake you. God may decide to test the faithfulness of a worshiper through any means; the worshipper will still be faced with the choice to take the test in good faith or not.

Joseph: The Worshipper's Insight into Dreams

Many worshippers are groomed in times of oppression, and sometimes they are sent to go and make way for the works and the people of the Lord. Joseph was sent ahead to go make preparation for the famine of the future. Worshippers are leaders, but not all leaders are worshippers.

Joseph had a foundation of attracting envy, jealousy and hate. He also attracted his master's wife who falsely accused him, which led to his imprisonment. The fear of God sent him into prison but he would rather fear God than men.

One major attribute that is universal in worship is the fear of God. This is why you see a worshipper looking back at their old lives lived in sin, they break down in tears all over again. The fear of God Joseph had revelation and insights into dreams. He was a dream, and he was given deep meanings of the dreams of others. He translated two major dreams to the closest aides of the king while they were in the same prison. Two years later, he was called to translate the Pharaoh's strange dream. And the following revelation was given to Joseph by the Lord.

Genesis 41:29-36 NKJV

Indeed seven years of great plenty will come throughout all the land of Egypt; but after them seven years of famine will arise, and all the plenty will be forgotten in the land of Egypt; and the famine will deplete the land. So the plenty will not be known in the land because of the famine following, for it will be very severe. And the dream was repeated to Pharaoh twice because the thing is established by God, and God will shortly bring it to pass. "Now therefore, let Pharaoh select a discerning and wise man, and set him over the land of Egypt. Let Pharaoh do this, and let him appoint officers over the land, to collect one-fifth of the produce of the land of Egypt in the seven plentiful years. And let them gather all the food of those good years that are coming, and store up grain under the authority of Pharaoh, and let them keep food in the cities. Then that food shall be as a reserve for the land for the seven years of famine which shall be in the land of Egypt, that the land may not perish during the famine."

Joseph was given the rare access into heavenly decisions concluded in the court of God that would affect nations. The nations would go into severe famine for years and intelligence was released that laid down them prevention methods to stay unaffected during the famine. This led to Joseph's rise to power, because he was the only one in all of Egypt who carried the heaven's intelligence needed to avert a national disaster of famine.

Revelation belongs to God and only worshippers who fear the Lord are given revelation: The fear of God is the beginning of wisdom, and the fear of the Lord was one of the reasons Joseph was given the mysteries of dreams.

Judah

Praise, Worshipper who repented and loved
genuinely his brother

Major Assignments

Led Israel into the promised land

Led Israel into many victors

The tribe where Jesus came from

10

JUDAH

LOVE & SACRIFICE WAS FLOWED FROM JUDAH'S HEART

> *"So please, my lord, let me stay here as a slave instead of the boy, and let the boy return with his brothers. For how can I return to my father if the boy is not with me? I couldn't bear to see the anguish this would cause my father!"*
> **GENESIS 44:30-34 NKJV**

Judah's Beginnings

Unlike Joseph, Judah's was born by a woman who was not the preferred wife of his father. His mother was not the preferred wife of Jacob his father. His mother, Leah, an unloved wife, seeing how the Lord had favored her in child bearing called her fourth son Judah. When Judah was born, Leah praised God for the birth of Judah, hoping his birth would win her the love of her husband. Judah's birth didn't bring improvements.

The boy Judah as a child did not show any indication of praise from the beginning of his life. He lived his life in hate, rebellion and strife. How then was Judah transformed from a darky and lowly dunghill into God's lawmaker, a national warleader, and the tribe which the Son of God brought forgiveness through. Judah was one of Joseph's brothers. His played a significant part in sending Joseph into slavery. When the other brothers were thinking of killing Joseph, Judah advised, *"Come and let us sell him to the Ishmaelites, and let not our hand be upon him, for he is our brother and our flesh."* - Genesis 37:27. His counsel was well received and Judah became the one who set the course of Joseph's life in captivity.

After selling out their brother, here's a picture of what happened and the story they presented to their father when they returned home.

Genesis 37:29-35

Then Reuben returned to the pit, and indeed Joseph was not in the pit; and he tore his clothes. And he returned to his brothers and said, "The lad is no more;and I, where shall I go?" So they took Joseph's tunic, killed a kid of the goats, and dipped the tunic in the blood. Then they sent the tunic of many colors, and they brought it to their father and said, "We have found this. Do you know whether it is your son's tunic or not?" And he recognized it and said, "It is my son's tunic. A wild beast has devoured him. Without doubt Joseph is torn to pieces." Then Jacob tore his clothes, put sackcloth on his waist, and mourned for his son many days. And all his sons and all his daughters arose to comfort him; but he refused to be comforted, and he said, "For I shall go down into the grave to my son in mourning." Thus his father wept for him.

There was their father at home who went into mourning as soon as he heard the reports that was given to him by his other sons including Judah

Proceeding With a Curse

A worshipper cannot build upon a foundation of rejection. Rejection and the feeling of being unloved does not translate into worship. A worshipper cannot get into their worship ministry without resolving their pasts with God. Without addressing his troubled foundation, Judah enters into his future accursed. If Judah had known how his family would be wiped away suddenly, he would not participate in trading Joseph's life. He got married and had 3 sons. Wickedness was found in his son and the Lord killed him; here's the first time Judah felt the pain of the loss of his loved one. He felt what he Jacob felt when he was told that a beast had devoured Jacob. Judah sought to preserve the memory of his late son. In desperation for an heir, he gets his younger son to give him the heir through Tamar, his late son's wife. Judah's second son Onan dealt deceitfully and was killed by the Lord. Next, Judah would not allow his last and only son, the only living blood relation to die like others, and he said to Tamar daughter-in-law, *"Remain a widow in your father's house till my son Shelah is grown." For he said, "Lest he also die like his brothers." And Tamar went and dwelt in her father's house* - Genesis **38:11**.

A Wrecked Destiny With a Prophetic Future

Anyone whose future is in worship must be aware that the satan intends to wreak havoc to mar their prophetic future. There comes a time when the kingdom of darkness comes requesting the season where the prophetic destiny of a worshipper is requested by the kingdom of darkness. How fragmented could Judah's life had gotten with the lost of 2 sons and his wife. His next descent was a bigger fall; bringing him into the lows which swallows no ordinary men - the deep pit of the strange woman. Genesis 38 reveals more of Judah's imperfection - making a promise he could not keep which got him into further trouble.

"Then Judah said to Tamar his daughter-in-law, "Remain a widow in your father's house till my son Shelah is grown." For he said, "Lest he also die like his brothers." And Tamar went and dwelt in

> *her father's house.   Now in the process of time the daughter of Shua, Judah's wife, died; and Judah was comforted, and went up to his sheep shearers at Timnah, he and his friend Hirah the Adullamite.   And it was told Tamar, saying, "Look, your father-in-law is going up to Timnah to shear his sheep." So she took off her widow's garments, covered herself with a veil and wrapped herself, and sat in an open place which was on the way to Timnah; for she saw that Shelah was grown, and she was not given to him as a wife. When Judah saw her, he thought she was a harlot, because she had covered her face.   Then he turned to her by the way, and said, "Please let me come in to you"; for he did not know that she was his daughter-in-law". - Genesis 36:12-16*

Tamar veils her identity when she heard Judah, her father-in-law was coming to town. She pretends to be a prostitute; and Judah fell for it. Judah and the prostitute of the moment got into a satanic negotiation.

> *"So she said, "What will you give me, that you may come in to me?" And he said, "I will send a young goat from the flock."So she said, "Will you give me a pledge till you send it?" Then he said, "What pledge shall I give you?" So she said, "Your signet and cord, and your staff that is in your hand." Then he gave them to her, and went in to her, and she conceived by him. So she arose and went away, and laid aside her veil and put on the garments of her widowhood" - Genesis 36:16-19*

Judah, ignorant of his destiny, gets into a transaction with the devil who had taken over Tamar. In exchange for sex, Tamar asked for a pledge as a payment - the items demanded as pledge was the signet, the cord and the staff in the hand of Judah. These items demanded were the three major items of utmost significance, symbolizing the prophetic destiny of Judah and these are their meanings.

1. **The Signet:** A signet is a very tiny seal usually as part of a ring of a person with high authority. It was mostly used as official stamps to mark documents as legal or official.

2. **The Cord :** The cord is a thread, signifying a bond and an agreement.

3. **The Staff:** The staff is a scepter, a symbol of authority and of power carried by royals.

Judah was in honor and he didn't know. He had no vision of his prophetic role in the future of a new nation. He had no clue that it would be declared concerning him - *"The scepter will not depart from Judah or the staff from between his feet until he whose right it is comes and the obedience of the peoples belongs to him."* - *Genesis 49:10*. Devil continues to use the same tactic to bring many down. At a time when individuals are unaware of their place in the kingdom of God, the devil comes to present them with a lie to steal the future from them.

Judah gave away all his symbol of authority and royalty, and entered into an act that reduces the destiny of many as Proverbs 26:6 says *"For by means of a harlot, a man is reduced to a crust of bread; And an adulteress will prey upon his precious life"*. Judah's actions rewrote his story. Many who are destined to worship have been destroyed in similar encounter. By the revelation of the Holy Spirit, we have learned that many whoo had a childhoood oof rejection usually get engaged is some form of unholy sexual relations at some point in their lives if they have not sought deliverance.

And Judah sent the young goat by the hand of his friend the Adullamite, to receive his pledge from the woman's hand, but he did not find her. Then he asked the men of that place, saying, "Where is the harlot who was openly by the roadside?" And they said, "There was no harlot in this place." So he returned to Judah and said, "I cannot find her. Also, the men of the place said there was no harlot in this place." Then Judah said, "Let her take them for herself, lest we be shamed; for I sent this young goat and you have not found her." And it came to pass, about three months after, that Judah was told, saying, "Tamar your daughter-in-law has played the harlot; furthermore she is with child by harlotry." So Judah said, "Bring her out and let her be burned!" When she was brought out, she sent to her father-in-law, saying, "By the man to whom these belong, I am with child." And she said, "Please determine whose these are—the signet and cord, and staff." So Judah acknowledged them and said, "She has been more righteous than I, because I did not give her to Shelah my son." And he never knew her again.

Attitudes of the Worshipper

Without worship, there is no good whatever in mankind. Quite often when people fall, they hardly take responsibility for the part they played in their fall, but they go ahead into accusation. God never looks at the gravity of sin, he looks at the willingness to humbly accept responsibility and repent. There is an uneasiness that comes upon the sinner when they are caught and exposed. The opening up of the sin of the sinner is one of the hardest encounter a singer goes through, but in that revelation is their deliverance from perdition.

When Judah was told her daughter-in-law was engaged in adultery and carrying a child - Judah was quoted saying *"let her be burned!"*, justifying the wicked and condemning the righteous. This is where many find themselves today, condemning others because their sins are covered. Judah eventually confessed the righteousness of Tamar. There are killers of worship, anyone who nurtures these killers will not enter into worship.

Killers of Worship

Killer #1: Swiftness in speech: Anyone who is careless in the use of word will get in trouble that will prevent them from entering into God's presence. Satan gets a high place in the life of those who speak carelessly.

Killer #2: Pride: Pride is the main reason holding people back from confession of sin and repentance.

Killer #3: Unrepentance: Many fail to successfully enter into worship because of their unrepentance nature. Many who worship today hide their sins, God does not allow for the mix up of holiness and filthiness.

Killer #4: Lovelessness : There is no worship without love. A person who does not love others cannot worship God. Judah had hate in him. He would not condemn his only son to death if situations were reversed, but he suggested Tamar be burnt.His recommendation gave insights into the state of his heart - a heart without love. 1 John 4:20 reminds us *Whoever claims to love God yet hates a brother or sister is a liar. For whoever does not love their brother and sister, whom they have seen, cannot love God, whom they have not seen.*
Worship cannot take place from a heart that is lacking love.
Anyone who has not met the Father cannot love the Son and cannot love human. When a man worshipper truly meets with the Lord, love is a visible fruit. They love not the world defines love now; they love genuinely and faithfully as God wants.

Leap into Worship

Submission: Judah's leap into worship came the moment he acknowledged and humbly declared *"She has been more righteous than I". Here is what God is asking every sinner to do when he says, "Come now, and let us reason together," Says the Lord, "Though your sins are like* scarlet, *They shall be as white as snow; Though they are red like crimson,* *They shall be as wool"* in Isaiah 1:18 NKJV. God doesn't want sinners to cover up sins, he doesn't want sinners to shift blames or get defensive, he wants to humbly accept our shortcomings - only then are we granted access into the company of his worshippers. At this point, Judah's heart was broken, but he knew it not just yet.

Love: The appointed came as decree from heaven to Pharaoh the king that there would be famine. There was famine everywhere, but there was none in Egypt. Jacob tells his children - the brothers of Joseph, Judah inclusive to go buy food in Egypt. They went to Egypt for the first time and found the favor of their brother who was the powerful leader over Egypt. The brothers returned the second time but this time with their little brother Benjamin. Judah had to convince his father before his father allowed him to send Judah along with them. For the first time in Judah's life, he loved selflessly

Genesis 48:8-10

"Then Judah said to Israel his father, "Send the boy along with me and we will go at once, so that we and you and our children may live and not die. I myself will guarantee his safety; you can hold me personally responsible for him. If I do not bring him back to you and set him here before you, I will bear the blame before you all my life. As it is, if we had not delayed, we could have gone and returned twice."

For the first time in his life, Judah was willing to give himself up for his brother, without expecting a payment. For the first time ever, love was found in Judah.

Intercession: They found favor a 2nd time with their brother. On their way back with their food purchase, Joseph's servants found a missing cup in their youngest brother's luggage. Just like their father had said, something happened that would prevent Benjamin from returning to his father. They were accused of theft, and Judah did the unexpected. He interceded for Benjamin their youngest brother and was willing to take his punishment. Out of all his brothers, he took upon the responsibility of sacrifice, a trait found in every worshipper and he interceded for his brother, for the love of his father and the love of his brother, preferring more than himself.

The Intercession of Judah
Genesis 44: 18-34 NKJV

Then Judah came near to him and said: "O my lord, please let your servant speak a word in my lord's hearing, and do not let your anger burn against your servant; for you are even like Pharaoh. My lord asked his servants, saying, 'Have you a father or a brother?' And we said to my lord, 'We have a father, an old man, and a child of his old age, who is young; his brother is dead, and he alone is left of his mother's children, and his father loves him.' Then you said to your servants, 'Bring him down to me, that I may set my eyes on him.' And we said to my lord, 'The lad cannot leave his father, for if he should leave his father, his father would die.' But you said to your servants, 'Unless your youngest brother comes down with you, you shall see my face no more.' "So it was, when we went up to your servant my father, that we told him the words of my lord. And our father said, 'Go back and buy us a little food. But we said, 'We cannot go down; if our youngest brother is with us, then we will go down; for we may not see the man's face unless our youngest brother is with us.' Then your servant my father said to us, 'You know that my wife bore me two sons; and the one went out from me, and I said, "Surely he is torn to pieces"; and I have not seen him since. But if you take this one also from me, and calamity befalls him, you shall bring down my gray hair with sorrow to the grave.' "Now therefore, when I come to your servant my father, and the lad is not with us, since his life is bound up in the lad's life, it will happen, when he sees that the lad is not with us, that he will die. So your servants will bring down the gray hair of your servant our father with sorrow to the grave. For your servant became surety for the lad to my father, saying, 'If I do not bring him back to you, then I shall bear the blame before my father forever.' Now therefore, please let your servant remain instead of the lad as a slave to my lord, and let the lad go up with his brothers. For how shall I go up to my father if the lad is not with me, lest perhaps I see the evil that would come upon my father?"

The time of Jesus here on earth was all about love. Jesus was given as a gift of love to mankind. There can be no true worship from a heart not given to love. Worship can only be poured out from a heart where love dwells. A selfless heart that seeks to give not because of what is expected to receive, but so that others can enjoy the benefit of what has been given. The generosity of the heart of Judah moved God. From this moment forward, the destiny of Judah in worship was sealed. The war against his place in worship ended forever. His lost seal, signet and cord were restored back to him. He was not only welcomed into the company of worshippers but he became the example and representation of worship. Wherever worship is mentioned in the Scriptures, the tribe symbolic to worship is Judah. Many great worshippers of the Scripture are from the tribe of Judah.

There are many Judah-like worshippers who never ended up as Judah because the enemy deceived them their sins were so grave that their worship would never matter to God. There are many drug addicts and prostitutes who would have worshipped like Judah, if they knew about the loving nature of God and the open admission into worship company of heaven and numberless possibilities of worship, sadly but they did not.

A Tribe of Warfare Praise

Judah became a fierce worship such that worship spread across his descendants and they became a tribe known for worship. The tribe of Judah are rugged worshippers. A tribe who marches into war in worship. Judah is a tribe who dances, rejoicing and worshipping and yet wars with swords in their hands. In all of Israel's war, Judah's praise leads Israel to war. All the fierce worshippers mentioned in the Scripture were from Judah. They war with one hand and worshipped with the other hand. Prophets like Isaiah, Joel, Habakuk, Daniel, Samuel, Zephaniah, Jeremiah, Nahum, Obadiah, Micah, Ezekiel were all from the tribe of Judah. Worship brings us closer to revelation and worship gains us victory.

This tribe is so special to God that God ordered that Judah be given an allotment of land closest to the entry of the tabernacle. Worshippers like David who was the first man to think of building God a house came from Judah. The worship of Judah was so delightful to the Father that God brought His Son through the tribe of praise. Forgiveness and salvation didn't come through any other way, but through the way of praise. This is how much worship means to God. No wonder God says a broken and a contrite heart He will not cast away.

Moses

Worshipper, Israel's Leader, Writer, Prophet, Friend of God

Instituted:

Received the designs of the Temple

The Feasts of the Lord,

Received & Re-Wrote The Law

Downloaded Israel's Purpose: A Holy Nation

Instituted the Priesthood As Revealed by Yahweh

11

MOSES

MOSES ASKS THE LORD FOR A NEW NAME

Then Moses said to God, "Indeed, when I come to the children of Israel and say to them, 'The God of your fathers has sent me to you,' and they say to me, 'What is His name?' what shall I say to them?" And God said to Moses, "I AM WHO I AM." And He said, "Thus you shall say to the children of Israel, 'I AM has sent me to you".

EXODUS 3:13

Walking with the Lord in worship brings the worshipper into having the privilege of an on-going conversation with the Lord. Our Lord is relational. There are a lot of information and knowledge He wants to release to the world. He will only pass knowledge through the worshipper. Moses was a worshipper; one whom the Lord entrusted with the history of the world, the story of the beginnings , the election of Israel as His inheritance, the laws, worship processes and His plan for the future.

Moses Fights the Battle of Worship

There's no worship without sacrifice. There is no worship without giving up a thing of high cost. The deeper the worship, the costlier the price of the sacrifice. Moses gave up a royal title, opted to leave the luxury of Pharaoh's palace to go on to live in simplicity. Moses' battle of worship began with him. He left the choice foods served in the palace, the royal treatments, and all the benefits that came with princely living. Then he encountered God and received the assignment to lead the Israelites out of Egypt for the purpose of worship. Ever worshipper gets to the opportunity to choose whether to worship God or save face, whether to please others. Moses chose to go with God genuinely and his decision was a very costly one.

The Revelations Given To Moses

The man Moses spent the majority of his older years receiving the history of the world and the plan for the future from the Lord. The Lord told Moses about how He created the world. The Lord told him about how He created light and how he separated it by day and night. The Lord told Moses about the creation of the trees, the animals and the creation of the man. The Lord told Moses about the establishment of the institution of marriage. The Lord told Moses about Adam and Eve. He told him about Cain and Abel, He told him about Noah and how He had once destroyed the world. Moses was one of the worshippers who had the most revelation in the Scriptures. In revelations given to Moses, we get to learn some of the mysteries of creation of mankind. In Genesis 2:7 - Moses shares the revelation

The Lord confided in Moses; He was a friend of God and He was elevated to the position of a god in front of Pharaoh. Moses was the worshipper with the longest revelation. Several times Moses would go up to the mountain fasting for 40 days, as the Lord downloads to him the history of the world, the happenings in the dawn of the world and things to come.

A conversation between God and Moses. During this conversation, God gave revelations to Moses about the name of God "YHWH" that had never been revealed to anyone before Him. Before Moses' encounter with the Lord. Abraham, Isaac, Jacob had encounters with the Lord. The Lord spoke to them, fellowship with them, but they knew the Lord as "God Almighty", but they had no clue that God Almighty has another name. To Moses, God said in Exodus 6:3 *"I appeared to Abraham, Isaac, and Jacob, as God Almighty, but by My name LORD I was not known to them.".* What the Lord is saying is that - You don't quite understand what you not will need me for but I will be there e for whatever you need me to be. The Lord entrusts secrets, opens up unheard mysteries to His worshippers. Moses spent most of His time in leadership in God's presence, receiving revelation, and writing down the laws, and plans for generations to come. This is what is available in worship.

Worship in Lifestyle

Moses worshipped the Lord in all his entirety. He also worshipped the Lord in His leadership. He was a very meek man - his meekness was translated as gentleness. Moses was described as meek - his meekness was translated as gentleness, kindness and humility by the Amplified Classic version of the Bible.

Numbers 12:3

Now the man Moses was very meek (gentle, kind, and humble) or above all the men on the face of the earth).

The gift of gentleness is found in worshippers who go far in the depths of worship. In gentleness there is peace, there is calmness, there is softness and quietness. A worshipper who will move in the prophetic realm will require the gift of gentleness. They will have a calm and gentle spirit as Moses. In working effectively under the revelation of Jesus, a great level of gentleness is required. A lousy or noisy soul cannot break through into the heart of God. *"Be still and know that I am Lord"* - Psalm 46:1 says. There will always be situations in the worshipper's life that looks like gentleness would not resolve, here's why God says to be still.

From the life of Moses, we must also realize that a known strength can be a point of attack and accusation for the enemy in the life of a worshipper. Moses had been identified as *a meek man,* above every other person on earth.

Moses' frustration with the Israelites would later lead him into a blunder where he acted in anger; an action that cost him the inheritance of the promiseland and almost cost him entry into the Kingdom of God after he departed the world. Moses was described as meek - his meekness was translated as gentleness, kindness and humility by the Amplified Classic version of the Bible.

Numbers 20:10-12 NKJV

"Hear now, you rebels! Must we bring water for you out of this rock?" Then Moses lifted his hand and struck the rock twice with his rod; and water came out abundantly, and the congregation and their animals drank. Then the Lord spoke to Moses and Aaron, "Because you did not believe Me, to hallow Me in the eyes of the children of Israel, therefore you shall not bring this assembly into the land which I have given them.

Because of the worshipper's closer relationship with the Father, there are higher expectations for the worshipper from the Lord. The worshipper has been granted revelations of the knowledge and glory of the Lord. The worshipper has been shown the love of the Father, hence the Lord sets the bar higher for His worshippers such that there is no allowance for any act that will bring dishonor to the name of their Father by whom they have been called by.

Ways of Worship

Many are the encounters of the worshipper, and sacrifice is definitely one of it.

Way #1: Pioneer: Good sends worshippers to pioneer new missions. For Moses, it started by the burning bush. A worshipper never doubts the voice of God. When Moses heard it, though he was afraid, he yielded to the strange assignment.

Way #1: Unconditional love: A worshipper loves much. Moses loved a group of people who proved difficult to love. The Israel camp wronged Moses in their ways and words, but Moses loved. At some point, Moses siblings, Aaron and Miriam rose against Moses in words, Moses prevailed in love.

Way #2: Intercession: When God didn't find people worthy of His favor, God was set to destroy them and start again with Moses; Moses stood in the way of God.

Way #3: Journaling: A worshipper encounters God in the most unlikely places and multiple times in a moment. Writing is one of the ways of worship. A worshipper wants to preserve the revelation, and the presence of God through words. A worshipper wants to share powerful encounters. Moses wrote extensively. He wrote the first 5 books of the Bible; Genesis, Exodus, Numbers, Leviticus, and Deteronomy. Like Moses, worshippers are custodians of God's revelation and secrets. They write down the policies of God and are agents.

Way #4: Leadership by service: A worshipper is a leader, whether they have a title or not. Leadership has nothing to do with titles. Moses was one of those leaders whose leadership role was visible to others. In leadership, a worshipper is distinguished through their service. Some leaders lead for benefits, while others do for God's purpose to be fulfilled; the latter is the worshipper.

From Moses' life, we find that the privilege to worship the Lord is given to us in all areas of our lives. Some will be given the opportunities to worship by the words they write, some by the people they lead, some by interceding for others. It all delights God if we commit our doings unto Him.

Noah

Worshipper, Friend of God who was righteous and lived in obedience

Instituted:

Noah's Ark

The Covenant with the Rainbow

Offered worship that saved humanity from subsequent
water destruction

12

NOAH

THE WORSHIP THAT CHANGED THE WORLD

Then Noah built an altar to the Lord, and took of every clean animal and of every clean, and offerings burnt offering on the atar. And the Lord smelled a soothing aroma.

GENESIS 8:20-21

There was one worship that changed the world, it was Noah's worship. It would still have been that God would wipe out the entire earth in His wrath everytime that iniquity abounds in the world, and leave only a few persons and animals behind, but Noah's worship overturned that.

When all the people of the world went rogue, one person stayed faithful. The story of Noah revisits a powerful event in history. The time when there was fullness of evil and God wiped out the entire world with water, leaving only one family behind. Why did God spare one family out of all the families in the world at the time? Noah was the leader of the spared family. Noah's worship was the worship that changed the mind of God and God declared;

Genesis 8: 20-21 NKJV

Then Noah built an altar to the Lord, and took of every clean animal and of every clean bird, and offered burnt offerings on the altar. And the Lord smelled a soothing aroma. Then the Lord said in His heart, "I will never again curse the ground for man's sake, although the imagination of man's heart is evil from his youth; nor will I again destroy every living thing as I have done.

Noah's Costly Worship

To the worshipper, the cost of worship is ultra expensive. Noah's worship was one of the costliest in the history of mankind. It was the beginning of a new world. All the clean animals that had been preserved were offered to God. To the carnal mind, Noah's act was illogical. How could Noah let go of all the clean animals? Is that not the reason why they were preserved by God? Noah did not withhold all that was left to begin a new world with, he let it all go, in worship. Noah is a worshipper to be studied. Here are some of the traits of worship found in Noah's lifestyle.

Noah: Traits of the worshipper

Trait #1 Hearing God's voice: The worshipper is privileged to hear from God. When God seals up revelation, when He hides His ways and plans from all others, He gives grace to the worshipper, and lays bare His heart to His worshippers. The mind of the worshipper positions the worshipper to hear from God. The mind of the worshipper is set on the things of God.

Trait #2 Obedience: Noah obeyed. He didn't doubt God. He simply followed God's instructions. The magnitude of the instruction given to Noah was enormous, so was the consequence. One of the major reasons why God stops speaking to people is disobedience to past instructions. When people refuse to listen to God's instructions, He stops giving new revelation. It was impossible for people to believe. They simply did not because such had never occurred before. Noah's obedience was in worship through faith. Outside of worship and faith, it's not easy for any man to go out to declare such warning, but Noah did regardless.

Trait #2 Focus : It is dangerous to abandon God's assignment just because growth is not perceived. The devil seeks to dissuade from consistency powered by the Holy Spirit. The worshipper must always stay focused and continue to build the ship God has given to them.

Trait #3 Faithfulness: Noah faithfully followed God's instructions. Noah preached repentance 100 years, though the people refused to listen. Noah's faithfulness was unwavering. His message was to warn about the upcoming disaster and get them into the place of safety. No one listened, apart from his family.

The Covenant with Noah, Marked with the Rainbow

Genesis 9:12-16 NKJV

And God said: "This is the sign of the covenant which I make between Me and you, and every living creature that is with you, for perpetual generations: I set My rainbow in the cloud, and it shall be for the sign of the covenant between Me and the earth. It shall be, when I bring a cloud over the earth, that the rainbow shall be seen in the cloud; and I will remember My covenant which is between Me and you and every living

creature of all flesh; the waters shall never again become a flood to
destroy all flesh. The rainbow shall be in the cloud, and I will look on it
to remember the everlasting covenant between God and every living
creature of all flesh that is on the earth."

After the flood, Noah's response was worship. Noah picked out the best animals for sacrifice. Noah's worship pleased the Lord and there was a new pact signed with humanity because of Noah's Sacrifice. Worship changed the heart of God that he took away the curse that was upon the earth - Genesis 7:20:21. Any worship that delights God brings about the establishment of a new covenant. New and eternal covenants are released after a worshipper offers acceptable worship. When men and women of old worshipped the Lord wholeheartedly, God issues new covenants.

As a sign of the covenant, God gave a sign - the rainbow. Like an earthly agreement, whenever two parties sign a contract, each party gets their copy. The rainbow is a complete circle around the throne of God. Half of the rainbow is displayed over the cloud as a reminder of God's covenant made with the human race because of the worship Noah offered and the other half of the rainbow in heaven.

Revelation 4:3 NKJV

And He who sat there was like a jasper and a sardius stone in
appearance; and there was a rainbow around the throne, in appearance
like an emerald.

In Revelation quoted above, the Scripture says there was a rainbow around the throne. The rainbow doesn't wrap around the throne unless it encircles the throne. Anytime the rainbow comes on earth, only half shows up and the other half is forms a half circle around God's throne, and is as a memorial of the covenant.

Worshippers are Lawmakers

When a nation is lost in of chronic iniquity, the ears of people are deafened to the gospel and cities are by the edge of heaven's wrath, the soul of a worshipper may be sufficient to overturn disaster. The faithful yielding of one person into the call of worship is all that is needed. Like the time of Noah, God can transform communities because of the sacrifice of a worshipper. A nation can be transformed because of the offering of a worshipper. And He can make new laws, laws that was never thought to be possible.

Worshippers are Builders

Genesis 9:20 NKJV

Now the sons of Noah who went out of the ark were Shem, Ham, and Japheth. And Ham was the father of Canaan. These three were the sons of Noah, and from these the whole earth was populated. And Noah began to be a farmer, and he planted a vineyard.

God said to me, "have you ever wondered what happened after the destruction of the world by water"? The answer to this question was found in Genesis 9:20 where God said, Noah became a farmer. A farmer is one who tills the land, plant crops, and also raises animals. Noah's role as a farmer was not quite an easy one. He had to plant for the new world to feed. Noah wasn't in Adam's shoes where God had done all the planting and all Adam had to do was the works of care and management. Noah's reality was different. Together with his family, they did the works of reconstruction and. replanting. Worshippers are resourceful builders and pioneers, used by God in the works of development of a people, a place, a community or nations. Every worshipper is called to build in some way.

Abraham

Worshipper, Friend of God

Remembered for:

Willingness to offer his only son to God

Celebrated first passover

Tithing to Melchizedek

13

ABRAHAM

---

3 DAYS TRAVEL TO OFFER HIS SON IN WORSHIP

"So Abraham rose early in the morning and saddled his donkey, and took two of his young men with him, and Isaac his son; and he split the wood for the burnt offering, and arose and went to the place of which God had told him. Then on the third day Abraham lifted his eyes and saw the place afar off".

GENESIS 22:3-4 NKJV

Abraham's Background In Idolatry

Abraham was a descendant of Noah. After Noah worship, soon after the works of rebuilding the nations began, sin and curse crept back into the world as soon as Noah got drunk and his son, Ham saw his nakedness. This incident, the drunkenness of a worshipper, set the rebuilding of the nation backwards. Though Noah's family continued to multiply, but right from the time of Noah's drunkenness, human wickedness resumed and multiplied. The evil had increased that men were determined and focused on building towers into the heavens. They had fallen back into the Lucifer's state of mind - wanting to steal God's glory and make a name for themselves.

This evil continued, but God's covenant with Noah held the hand of God against destroying the earth a second time. People continued in their atrocious acts. It was out of this darkness that Abraham's father, Terah was led out by the Lord and set upon the journey to Haran, however, Terah never made it to the set destination.

Satan's Perversion of the Rainbow

An overflow of evil from the time of Noah was the perversion of the rainbow. It was far from God's delight when a U.S. presidency lit the rainbow and called it gay pride. God said, "the enemy had orchestrated that to chase out the glory of God from the United States". God owns the rainbow, the first time the rainbow was released to signify and provide a reminder of the covenant made with all flesh. Scientifically, the rainbow is found to be some kind of splitting of a light source going through a reflective index medium and splitting its colors. When God made this covenant with Noah, it was not a covenant made in darkness or a covenant of darkness, it was a covenant made publically in light with God saying - I made a covenant with you that I will not destroy the earth with water. Only worshippers can break the chain of this perversion and association of the rainbow with the gay movement.

Abraham's Call to Worship

Terah's country of birth was so full of evil, but the existing covenant made with Noah hindered God from eliminating evil from the world. God made a better way, He called Terah's son, Abraham entirely out of the idolatrous country for God to begin a new nation of worshippers. God says to Abraham, formerly called Abram;

Genesis 9:20 NKJV

The Lord had said to Abram, "Go from your country, your people and your father's household to the land I will show you. "I will make you into a great nation, and I will bless you; I will make your name great, and you will be a blessing. I will bless those who bless you, and whoever curses you I will curse; and all peoples on earth will be blessed through you..

Battle for Worship

There comes a time where the worship will have to make a choice and battle for worship. There is never standing in between. The worshipper requires a clear, broad and distinct separation from darkness, from all ways of old. Hardly will any worshipper continue association with idolatrous family altars and successfully worship the Lord. Only a few can work in this breakthrough of obedience.

Battle #1: Goodbye to the Old: There is never a mix and match with God. There is no worshipper who sets out to worship God that is not called out of the older ways. Usually some relationships that will hinder worship will be ended, and some doors will be shut for worship to advance. This is a battle for worship. Abraham had to leave his country, his people, his father's household and everything behind, and go into the unknown.

In our prophetic ministry journey, some of the reasons why worshippers lay dormant in perpetual affliction is holding on to the old. This battle is one of the toughest and only a few, very few people win this battle. Unfortunately, anyone who disobeys and hangs on to the old ways.

Battle #2: Radical faith: A worshipper worships in a different kind of faith. It is radical faith. God releases the entire plan to the worshipper. Then in navigation, only the road to the next destination on the map is released to the worshipper and God awaits obedience. After obedience, the journey continues. Abraham set out into a place unknown. This is radical faith. The worship of the worshipper becomes more delightful to God with such a massive faith, and it pleases God.

Battle #3: The Journey of Worship: Abraham will not worship in mediocrity,and will give all it takes to get to the site of worship, even when the object of the worship was his only son. When a man waits until his old age before the heir to his empire is born; then He hears from God to go offer him in worship to the Lord. What does he do? Abraham journeyed for 3 days to the place of sacrifice. The way of worship is very costly. A worshipper will not withhold anything from the Lord.

Isaac: The Son Who Submitted

At the time of Abraham's journey to worship God with his only son Isaac, Isaac was possibly in his early teenage years. He knew when they are going for sacrifice, they carried along the wood, and all the other needed items for the sacrifice. Yet Isaac asked, "Father where is the lamb". Isaac knew the way of worship. He knew a lamb was needed, but there was no lamb in view. Isaac could have disappeared into thin air, afterall his father was an old man who may not be able to run as fast as he could. However, IIsaac surrendered to the will of his own father who was surrendering to the will of the Heavenly Father. No wonder was Isaac the child of promise. The child of covenant did not struggle, but surrendered to the will of his father.

Worship, Prophecy, Grace, Mercy and Intercession

Abraham was a worshipper, an intercessor, and a man filled with the grace and mercy of the Most High. As with Abraham; anyone who breaks through into worship also breaks through into intercession. In the sphere of worship and intercession, grace and mercy is released upon the life of the worshiper.

Intercessors are Heaven's diplomats and lawmakers of YHWH on earth. When decrees are established in heaven; intercessors on earth can stand before the Lord and present their reasons for the Lord to change His mind and not bring destruction upon the lives of sinners. There is deep integration between Worship, intercession, grace and mercy. Without worship there is no intercession. Worship, being diverse in description, has been described as the contriteness of heart, the humility of heart, because without humility there is no worship.

Intercession & Grace

In Abraham's life was an abundance of grace. There were countless favor upon his life and he also had righteousness imputed upon him. A person lacking in grace cannot stand before God to intercede for others. God is just, fair and true to His word. Before God does a thing; He confides in His friends. That still continues upon until right now. He confides in intercessors about upcoming plans for the people, cities, nations whether good or bad. He tells of the evil that has been wrecked and tells His intercessors the things that are to unfold.

The grace of God can overturn judgment upon the lives of a people. In the case of Sodom and Gomorrah; the grace upon Abraham had no jurisdiction over the city facing the judgement of destruction from the Lord. Abraham and the Lord gets into a conversation:

Genesis 18:26-32 NKJV

"If I find in Sodom fifty righteous within the city, then I will spare all the place for their sakes." "If I find there forty-five, I will not destroy it." I will not do it for the sake of forty." I will not do it if I find thirty there." "I will not destroy it for the sake of twenty." "I will not destroy it for the sake of ten." So the Lord went His way as soon as He had finished speaking with Abraham; and Abraham returned to his place.

For a city set for destruction, Abraham estimated there ought to be 50 whose grace would be sufficient for the entire city; but it was not so. He estimated there would be at least 45, but there was none, and then he went down to 40, 30, and 20 and then 10. If there were 10 people found righteous, 10 people with a heart like Abraham's the grace upon their lives could have saved the entire city of Sodom and Gomorrah.

Abraham had a history of interceding with the Lord; although he could not get God to change His mind concerning Sodom and Gomorrah; but for the sake of Abraham, Israel still stands today. Israel's sin is no different from Gomorrah's evil. But why was one chosen and favored and one utterly destroyed from the surface of the earth? There was a worshipper who was an intercessor who received vast amount of God's grace and His mercy. The spirit of worship and intercession in the life of Abraham is upon the remnant seed of Israel until this moment. The intercession of Abraham was a blessing such that it was written:

Romans 9:29 NKJV

"Unless the lord Sabaoth had left us a seed, We would have become like Sodom and we would have been made like Gomorrah

Every intercessor is a worshipper. Those who intercede at no cost, praying over peoples, communities and nations even when there seem to be no return on investment, but out of God's pure love.

Jonathan

Worshipper who saw wrong and called it wrong

Remembered for:

His brotherly sacrifice

His friendship with David

14

JONATHAN

JONATHAN - THE WORSHIPPER WHO LOVES...

"And Jonathan made a solemn pact with David, because he loved him as he loved himself. Jonathan sealed the pact by taking off his robe and giving it to David, together with his tunic, sword, bow, and belt."

1 SAMUEL 18:3-4 NLT

He was the heir to the throne of Israel, until his father did a great disservice to the God of Israel. He was next in line to become the king of Israel. He was kind hearted; he had the heart of a shepherd. He would not call right wrong, He would not call wrong right, even if the one on the wrong side was his father. He was a prince who had the heart of a servant. There was no pride found in him. In war his hand was strengthened. He was a friend. He was a man of his words and a man who placed a hefty price on his covenants. In him, we see the image of the Lord Jesus that would come generations after. He laid down the essence of his heirship, in a submission to the will of the Lord, so that his best friend would ascend the throne. The story of Jonathan was one of worship, sacrifice and pure love.

Worship is a journey into the heart of God. The goal is that the heart of the worshipper becomes knit with the heart of God. Instead of the worshipper thinking about "me", "I, "myself", the heart of the worshipper knits with the Lord. The first earthly experience of this is what was experienced between David and Jonathan. It came as a result of a conversation - *And it came to pass, when he had made an end of speaking unto Saul, that the soul of Jonathan was knit with the soul of David, and Jonathan loved him as his own soul* - 1 Samuel 18:1.

A Knitted Soul in Worship

There was a divine transfer as they exchanged their garments. Rightfully the throne belonged to Jonathan. His life was a symbol of the life of Jesus. He was a valiant warrior. On the account of Jonatahn, the Lord brought victory to all Israel. Although the Lord had anointed David to become the next king but he would not become king for quite a number of years to come. Jonathan gave him the kingdom in the exchange of the garments. It was a secret exchange where the garment took place. No one knew in the royal family about the kingdom that Jonathan had handed over to his friend. The death that Jesus would come and die on calvary. The description of the life and death of Jonathan was described in the book of John 15 - greater love than no love than this that a man would lay his life for his friend. That was what Jonathan did . It was a greater deeper bond of friendship.

David described the kind of love as a love more than the love of a woman. The love that flows from the core of the heart of a worshipper is beyond the love of a man to woman or a woman to man. It is beyond the fusion of the relationship that exists between a man and a woman. Even though God is the orginitor of marital bliss and copulation, yet the love in the heart of a worshipper is beyond these. This is why the prayer of Jesus before he left the earth was very paramount. Jesus prayed in John 17:21, *I pray that they will all be one, just as you and I are one—as you are in me, Father, and I am in you. And may they be in us so that the world will believe you sent me.*

Battle for Worship

Jonathan fought the rarest type of battle for worship. His battle had expensive and sacrificial.

Battle #1: Gave up His Inheritance: Jonathan caught the revelation early on that God didn't intend to continue the rulership of Israel under the reign of His father, Saul. He knew God has given the kingdom into the hand of David. The kingdom was expected to be passed down Jonathan, but Jonathan's response was strange. The Scripture says in 1 Samuel 18: 4 - *Jonathan took off the robe he was wearing and gave it to David, along with his tunic, and even his sword, his bow and his belt.* Jonathan handed over his future throne to the future king, without the knowledge of Saul or any other person from the royal family. They could have killed him for handing over the throne. All that Jonathan handed to David was the symbol the entire essence of the kingship of Israel, the authority, the throne and all the power that comes with it. There was no way that Jonathan would be alive and David would become king. Long before his death, Jonathan prepared David for the throne. No wonder David said after he later heard of Jonathan's death in 2 Samuel 1:26 *"I am distressed for you, my brother Jonathan; very pleasant have you been to me. Your love to me was wonderful, passing the love of women."* These words, coming from David, a man who had encounters with different women knew what sacrificial love was, and he experienced that with Jonathan his friend, brother, the son of his greatest enemy.

Battle #3: Uncompromisingly Truthful: Filled with truth and would not bend the truth. He said to his father Saul, *Jonathan spoke well of*

David to Saul his father and said to him, "Let not the king do wrong to his servant David; he has not wronged you, and what he has done has benefited you greatly. 5 He took his life in his hands when he killed the Philistine. The Lord won a great victory for all Israel, and you saw it and were glad. Why then would you do wrong to an innocent man like David by killing him for no reason?" - 1 Samuel 19:4-5. At a time that Saul could have ordered that Jonathan's life be taken alongside David. Out of David's presence, Jonathan spoke the truth clearly without mincing words, or playing around safety.

Battle #2: Faithfulness in Friendship: When Saul sought to take the life of David, Jonathan remained faithful, saying to David, *"My father Saul is looking for a chance to kill you. Be on your guard tomorrow morning; go into hiding and stay there. I will go out and stand with my father in the field where you are. I'll speak to him about you and will tell you what I find out."- 1 Samuel 19:2-3* This act of righteousness is only possible from a heart that worships. Jonathan remained faithful to his friendship with David.

Worshippers like Jonathan are the worshippers who go through the sufferings with Jesus. Worshippers like Jonathan are dedicated to God's cause without looking to the left or right, they are solely focused on putting in their all to fulfill God's mission, even if it seem to place them in a place of loss in human terms.

David

Worshipper, Warrior, king of Israel,   Inventor, father of the Lord Jesus, Musician, Prophet, Author

Instituted:

247 worship

First thought of building a house for God

Functional Areas:

An inventor of music instruments

Leader who builds others

Prophet who prophesied and worked in the Holy Spirit before the Holy Spirit

was made available to all

15

DAVID

KING DAVID'S DESIRE TO BUILD GOD'S HOUSE

> Now it came to pass when the king was dwelling in his house, and the Lord had given him rest from all his enemies all around, that the king said to Nathan the prophet, "See now, I dwell in a house of cedar, but the ark of God dwells inside tent curtains.
>
> **2 SAMUEL 7:1-2 NKJV**

As a young forgotten boy who rose from the role of a shepherd, into Israel's greatest king and moved the heart of God into one of the most powerful covenants ever; A shepherd, a youngest child with the right heart before God, one of the greatest kings of Israel, the father to the wisest son.....and a man who walked into one of the greatest covenants ever with the Lord through His works. The

ETERNAL KING, JESUS CHRIST came through David. Worship flowed too God from David's heart such that God made an eternal covenant with him

2 Samuel 7:13 NKJV

When your days are fulfilled and you lie down with your fathers, I will raise up your offspring after you, who shall come from your body, and I will establish his kingdom. He shall build a house for my name, and I will establish the throne of his kingdom forever..

How did David earn so much favor before God? How did a shepherd melt the heart of God, moving God to call him a "man after his own heart". Jesus Christ, God's only son, was sent through the lineage of King David because of this covenant. Jesus was notably called **"Son of David"**. When referring to His origin, He was called, **"Offspring of David"**, **"Rod Out of the Stem of Jesse"**, **"Root of David"**. The Messiah that came to save the whole world, came out of the very root of King David. Learning the ways of David is a powerful eye-opener that will help you in your own journey in life, and also help you be a partaker of the Davidic blessings and impact your generations for years to come. In this study, we are looking at how the heart of a man, created a special love between him and God, how through his heart, his attitude, his personality, he created not just a seat, but a lasting throne for his generation in the presence of God. How he left a kingly inheritance for his offspring. Any worshipper can be drafted into the covenant of David by change of attitude, holiness,by wearing the garment of humility, by putting on the apparel of wisdom and by yielding to the Lord completely genuinely. A worshipper can establish new covenants between them and God in the order of David.

The Making of a Rare Worshipper

There are a group of worshippers who are born out of slavery, rejection and loneliness. David falls into this group. Growing up, he was an outcast in the Jesse family. Planted deep in family slavery, and had no connection with love. Worshippers may be made from seasons of trials, deep worshippers are made through from the furnace. Some hardships are allowed by God to break and shape the worshipper. The life of a worshipper may be lonely because many friendships do not align with the cost of worship. David's early life was lived in rejection and loneliness.

The road to worship was long for David. It was not 6 months, 1 year, or 2 years of 3 years that David spent at the backyard taking care of the sheep. All he woke up to see everyday was the backside of the sheep. He learned all the lessons for life with the sheep. He diligently did his job as a shepherd. When the lions showed up, he conquered it in protection of the sheep. When the deer showed up, he killed it. In his wilderness journey, he was given a two-fold mantle; the mantle of praise and worship. On his front, he wore an apparel of thanksgiving, and around him at the back, he wore gratitude as his garment. He was from Judah. His forefather was Abraham, Isaac and Jacob. Worship was his lifestyle. Worship was his attitude. Worship was the condition of the heart. On his head was the hat of humility. He was so close to God that God called him, "a man after my heart". There was that time when David also fought the battle for worship.

David's Battle for Worship

This is a battle any worshipper cannot avoid. It is a battle every worshipper fights at every point. Abraham fought it, he left his home, his convenience and went into a place he knew nothing about, in submission to the Lord. Job fought it, he lost all that he had because he was a worshipper. Moses fought it, he refused to allow his people to suffer in slavery and led a national deliverance despite teh unwilingness of the people. Daniel fought it in the battle of worship in Babylon when he boldly brought the name of Yahweh into a region where the name of God was forbidden. The 3 Hebrew brothers fought the battle of worship. The Apostles and the early church fought it.

It got to David's turn to fight the fight of worship when he was sent on a routine assignment to deliver food to his brother. He heard about Goliath's oppression.

1 Samuel 17:25-26 NKJV

Now the Israelites had been saying, "Do you see how this man keeps coming out? He comes out to defy Israel. The king will give great wealth to the man who kills him. He will also give him his daughter in marriage and will exempt his family from taxes in Israel." David asked the men standing near him, "What will be done for the man who kills this Philistine and removes this disgrace from Israel? Who is this uncircumcised Philistine that he should defy the armies of the living God?".

After David said these, he might have thought in his mind. *"you cannot ridicule my father like this"* . This came at a time when Israel was under oppression and shame. With a heart full of worship, David rose up in the face of a critical battle with the mighty. With no military experience or formal training, David fought and won Goliath.

David's Lifestyle Before the Fight

Trait #1: Worship in the wilderness

David had taken the time in the secret place communing with the Lord. He was trained in the wilderness, and had mastered stillness and quietness of the soul. He probably talked to himself a lot too. He had trained his spiritual ears and mouth to be able to hear from the Lord and the Spirit of God was upon him. It got to a place that the word of God had grown in His life than in the life of the king of israel and the entire army of Israel. David's time with God in the wilderness had nurtured him into a fierce worshipper, who carries God's authority and power. As with most ancient worshippers, they had been long lost in worship in God's presence long before their unveiling. There would not have been a public ministry for David without a private worship ministry. As with David, we must be reminded that we may be worship ministers who organizes worship meetings, the majority of our worship ministry is not conducted in front of a crowd, but in a one-on-one with the Most High.

Trait #2: Extreme Humility
David's heart was humble and set right before God. David was broken, and there was no self-exaltation on his heart. He had been through the lowest of lows. He was relegated to the wilderness, and he took his duties with joy.

Trait #3: Focused
David's mind was made up and his eyes were set on Israel's deliverance. He refused to be swayed with negativity, even when it came from within his household: *When Eliab, David's oldest brother, heard him speaking with the men, he burned with anger at him and asked, "Why have you come down here? And with whom did you leave those few sheep in the wilderness? I know how conceited you are and how wicked your heart is; you came down only to watch the battle." "Now what have I done?" said David. "Can't I even speak?" He then turned away to someone else and brought up the same matter, and the men answered him as before. What David said was overheard and reported to Saul, and Saul sent for him -* I Samuel 17:28-21. David continued to research until he was given audience by the king Saul who would approve of his mission. A worshipper never focuses on the opinions of others, but on the mission God has sent them.

Trait #4: The Right Skill Sets
David didn't go to war in emptiness, he went full of experience. He went as one who knew how to apply what was in his hands to other situations. He sold his experience in fighting weird animals to Saul

and saul bought it. *Saul replied, "You are not able to go out against this Philistine and fight him; you are only a young man, and he has been a warrior from his youth." But David said to Saul, "Your servant has been keeping his father's sheep. When a lion or a bear came and carried off a sheep from the flock, I went after it, struck it and rescued the sheep from its mouth. When it turned on me, I seized it by its hair, struck it and killed it. Your servant has killed both the lion and the bear; this uncircumcised Philistine will be like one of them, because he has defied the armies of the living God. The Lord who rescued me from the paw of the lion and the paw of the bear will rescue me from the hand of this Philistine."* (I Samuel 17:28-21). Many times, God trains us in one type of war to have the skills to win other types of war. The worshipper must not underestimate whatever training God has taken them through.

Trait #5: Know & Master Your Tools for Life

Everyone is given a toolkit. In the toolkit of each one are tools for life. The tool for life are devices, objects, equipment, instruments, that God chose and ordained with us during our creation process, to be used as a part of the assignment we were sent here for. The worshipper must identify what their tools for life are and they must master how to use those tools. At some point in David's life, the enemy sought to trap him into using an armor kit that he was not familiar with. *Then Saul dressed David in his own tunic. He put a coat of armor on him and a bronze helmet on his head. David fastened on his sword over the tunic and tried walking around, because he was not used to them. "I cannot go in these," he said to Saul, "because I am not used to them." So he took them off. Then he took his staff in his hand, chose five smooth stones from the stream, put them in the pouch of his shepherd's bag and, with his sling in his hand, approached the Philistine.* (I Samuel 17:38-40). As soon as David realized, he said those were not the tools for him, he went for what was his; a staff, 5 stones, sling and shepherd's bag. And this brings us to the subject of worship identity to be discussed in subsequent sections of this chapter.

Trait #6: In God's Name

David was hidden in the name of the Lord. He went into war as a representative of God, not as himself. He said to Goliath, "I have come on this mission in God's name". Every mission the worshipper is sent out for must be in God's name, otherwise the worshipper is out on their own. *"David said to the Philistine, "You come against me with sword and spear and javelin, but I come against you in the name of the Lord Almighty, the God of the armies of Israel, whom you have defied. This day the Lord will deliver you into my hands, and I'll strike you down and cut off your head. This very day I will give the carcasses of the Philistine army to the birds and the wild animals, and the whole world will know that there is a God in Israel. All those gathered here will know that it is not by sword or spear that the Lord saves; for the battle is the Lord's, and he will give all of you into our hands."* David also remembered to calmly pass the message across to Goliath that it wasn't his battle, but the Lord's, this confidence could only come from having God's assurance of victory. (I Samuel 17:45-47).

Snares Against the worshipper

Snare #1: Praises from the People

Immediately David was given victory by God to win the battle for Israel, his first enemy was Saul the king because the people praised David more. Apart from making natural enemies when God begins to work miracles through the worshipper, there is a major caution to be aware of. When God begins to move mightily through the worshipper. One of the first snares set for the soul of the worshipper comes from the high praise directed at the worshipper by unsuspecting people who have experienced God's move. This snare is set by the devil to invoke pride with the knowledge of God's hatred for the proud.

Snare #2: Unexpected Internal Enemies

The worshipper can be ensnared by internal enemies who appear to have established a relationship with God, but in actual fact are far from the ways of God. Saul, the king of Israel unexpectedly became David's enemy. He became an unavoidable enemy, one whom David reports to, and the highest leader in Israel. The Scripture says; *Saul had a spear in his hand and he hurled it, saying to himself, "I'll pin David to the wall." But David eluded him twice.* (I Samuel 18:10-11).

Snare #3: The Snare of the Strange Woman or Strange Man

A major snare set against worshippers is the snare of the strange man or the strange woman. The first goal of this snare is to kill worship in the worshipper. Many worshippers are ensnared into the wrong marriage, and in most cases, that's the end of their worship. David was also ensnared *"Now Saul's daughter Michal was in love with David, and when they told Saul about it, he was pleased. "I will give her to him," he thought, "so that she may be a snare to him and so that the hand of the Philistines may be against him".* (I Samuel 18: 20-21). God favored David and turned his wife's heart towards him instead. However, there is one major problem with snares. Snares hardly ever forget their purposes. This was the case when Michal sought to silence David's worship long after Saul was dead.

After David became king, something major happened. *Now as the ark of the Lord came into the City of David, Michal, Saul's daughter, looked through a window and saw King David leaping and whirling before the Lord; and she despised him in her heart. So they brought the ark of the Lord, and set it in its place in the midst of the tabernacle that David had erected for it. Then David offered burnt offerings and peace offerings before the Lord. And when David had finished offering burnt offerings and peace offerings, he blessed the people in the name of the Lord of hosts. Then he distributed among all the people, among the whole multitude of Israel, both the women and the men, to everyone a loaf of bread, a piece of meat, and a cake of raisins. So all the people departed, everyone to his house. Then David returned to bless his household. And Michal the daughter of Saul came out to meet David, and said, "How glorious was the king of Israel today, uncovering himself today in the eyes of the maids of his servants, as one of the base fellows shamelessly uncovers himself! So David said to Michal, "It was before the Lord, who chose me instead of your father and all his house, to appoint me ruler over the people of the Lord, over Israel. Therefore I will play music before the Lord. And I will be even more undignified than this, and will be humble in my own sight. But as for the maidservants of whom you have spoken, by them I will be held in honor." Therefore Michal the daughter of Saul had no children to the day of her death.* (2 Samuel 6: 16-23). David's response determined whether David was for the Lord or for satan. He chose the worship of God, and not the worship of humans. This marked a new victory for Israel's great worshipper. One of the major lessons to be drawn from David and Michal's story is that opposition comes and it could come from the weakest link closest to the worshipper. Another lesson is that God destroys the fruitfulness of anyone who opposes His worship. There are more lessons to be learned based on related experiences God has brought into our radar in ministry.

There was the case of a seasoned worshipper and pastor who was in chronic affliction, and we prayed with him. I asked God what to pray about, God said -- HIS WIFE WAS A SNARE, HE CHOSE HIS WIFE OVER THE OIL I HAVE PLACED OVER HIS HEAD. Another instance, it was another worshipper of God. He had requested prayers, and I inquired of the Lord, the Lord said, -- HE IS NOT READY FOR DELIVERANCE OR TO HEAR THE TRUTH. HIS MOTHER IS THE ENEMY, SHE IS A WITCH, NOT READY TO REPENT & CLEVERLY HIDING BEHIND THE NAME OF JESUS. THERE IS NO MOVING FORWARD UNTIL HE WINS

THIS SPIRITUAL WAR. We never released the word. Whenever there is a compromise in the life of the worshipper, the Lord delivers the worshipper into the hands of the enemy. If David had thought of it to yield to the enemy speaking through Michal his wife, and become embarrassed to dance foolishly in worship, that would have marked the end of his relationship with God.

Many voices of worship has been silenced by the strange men and women of the world. One of the potent ways satan incapacitates the worshipper is through sexual covenants. Hence, satan's agents are trained to look for sexual commitments to lock the worshipper in. Once a worshipper is locked into a sexual covenant, the worshipper is hardly ever loosened, except God's radical deliverance mercy is released. This is the reason why there are many satanic agents, sent in the way of the worshipper.

Worship Identity

A worshipper must be familiar with their instruments of worship. Every worshipper is created with a main worship instrument as their worship tool for worship. That main worship is part of the worshipper's worship identity in heaven. David's main instrument was the harp, and it pleased God when he worshipped God on the harp.

Ezekiel 28:13 NIV

"You were in Eden, the garden of God; Every precious stone was your covering: The ruby, the topaz and the diamond; The beryl, the onyx and the jasper; The lapis lazuli, the turquoise and the emerald; And the gold, the workmanship of your settings and sockets, Was in you. On the day that you were created They were prepared."

David's worship had its uniqueness before God and he dared to make a bold statement about a vacuum that would be created in rendering praises to God if he dies.

To you, Lord, I called; to the Lord I cried for mercy:"What is gained if I am silenced, if I go down to the pit? Will the dust praise you? Will it proclaim your faithfulness?Hear, Lord, and be merciful to me; Lord, be my help."

Revelations of David

King David was Israel's most prominent king. David had revelations than a lot of his predecessors and successors. David is reported to have written about 73 out of 150 psalms. The life of David gave us the many revelations into different sides of God.

Worship: David was the great grandfather of 24-hour worship. He would go and sit down before God and start having extended conversation with the Lord. David had the word of God in him. He caught the revelations of worship very early. Sometimes believers are shouting and hurling commands at the Lord to respond to their prayers. Worship is the only currency in the presence of the Lord. Without being founded and grounded in the Word, the worshipper is misguided. When a worshipper is planted deep in the Word, then worship comes from the throne of grace, energized by the Holy Spirit, through the heart of men back into the throne of God. David understood that and said in Psalm 69, I will praise your name, this is better than any sacrifice.

The Messiah: David was given the revelation and he made the announcement of the coming of the Messiah into the world. The

Lord showed him the priesthood of Jesus, and he was quoted saying in Psalm 110; "You are a priest forever according to the order of Melchizedek".

The Revelation of Conception: King David was given a more precise explanation of what happens at the conception of the human. God said to Moses, that he made man with dust and breathe his breath upon man so man would become a living being. David got more details, in Psalm 139 especially between verses 13 and 16 - *For you formed my inward parts: you covered me in my mother's womb -My frame was not hidden from you. When I was made in secret And skillfully wrought in the lowest part of the earth. Your eyes saw my substance being yet unformed and in your book they all were written, The days fashioned for me, When as yet there were none of them.* Here are some Scriptures, revealing the creation of the soul of man, when the body had not yet been moulded by the potter, when God fashions the soul where no eyes were present.

Prophetic Prayers: In worship, prayers were opened up to David. When a man prays, he can still pray amiss. When a worshipper with the heart of the Lord worships, He cannot miss God. You are no longer seeking God when you're worshipping God. You are being sought by the Lord. It does not matter how many are in the place. The host of heaven come down and channels the praise back to the King of glory.

Psalm 23 NKJV

The LORD is my shepherd; I shall not want. He maketh me to lie down in green pastures; He leadeth me beside the still waters. He restoreth my soul; He leadeth me in the paths of righteousness for His name's sake. Yea, though I walk through the valley of the shadow of death, I will fear no evil; for Thou art with me; Thy rod and Thy staff, they comfort me. Thou preparest a table before me in the presence of mine enemies; Thou anointest my head with oil; my cup runneth over. Surely goodness and mercy shall follow me all the days of my life; and I will dwell in the house of the LORD forever."

With Psalm 23, David declare who God was in His life and his relationship to God. He explained how God cares for him and how he had been led safely in the most dangerous path. These are very powerful

Prophetic Healing: At a time when his boss, king Saul was demon-possed, spirit-filled David would play the harp and the demons would flee and Saul would receive healing.

Leadership: David carried an anointing to deliver the mind of people who were conditioned to failure. *David left Gath and escaped to the cave of Adullam. When his brothers and his father's household heard about it, they went down to him there. All those who were in distress or in debt or discontented gathered around him, and he became their commander. About four hundred men were with him.* (1 Samuel 22:1-2) As a worshipper, David was given the ability to take people from the dunghill and turn them into leaders who stand tall and represent nations. He came up with programs that transformed the rejected, the failed and the lowly of society into their leadership phases.

Sacrifices of David

The Thoughtfulness Offering:

Psalms 132:3-5 NIV

"Surely I will not go into the chamber of my house, Or go up to the comfort of my bed; I will not give sleep to my eyes Or slumber to my eyelids, Until I find a place for the LORD, A dwelling place for the Mighty One of Jacob."

The Water Offering: This worship began from a place of oppression and lack. David was very thirst. He had been disposed from home and he was longing for Bethlehem. He didn't know when he would see Bethlehem again. He thought aloud and spoke out, saying how much he missed the water he drank back home. Three of his mighty men volunteered to go get the choice water. His mighty men went to get the water, they had to break through the enemy camp, fought their way into Bethlehem, get the water and went through the same process on their way back to deliver the water to David, just to quench his thirst. These men learned loyalty from David. After the water was handed to him, David wouldn't drink the water, though he was thirsty, maybe dehydrated; he trembled and poured out the water unto God as an offering.

II Samuel 23:15-17 NKJV

"And David said with longing, "Oh, that someone would give me a drink of the water from the well of Bethlehem, which is by the gate!" So the three mighty men broke through the camp of the Philistines, drew water from the well of Bethlehem that was by the gate, and took it and brought it to David. Nevertheless he would not drink it, but poured it out to the LORD. And he said, "Far be it from me, O LORD, that I should do this! Is this not the blood of the men who went in jeopardy of their lives?" Therefore he would not drink it. These things were done by the three mighty men."

The Covenants God Made With David

God's relationship with David didn't end after David rested with his fathers. The relationship continued with his children, and continued with his tribe, nation and any worshipper that chooses the way of the Lord and devotes their entire life to the Lord..

The Key of David

In the entire history of the world, Israel is God's chosen people. Within Israel, Judah holds a very special place in God's heart; and within Judah, the house of David occupy a precious spot in God's heart. The King David was a man who went far into the extremes and reached the other end of worship that he became the representation of an institution where grace and mercy is established. This institution is called *The Key of David*. With the Key of David; there is access to the *covenant of the house of David, the throne of David* and *sure mercies of David*. This uniquely unusual key is entrusted in the hands of a select tested and approved worshippers. This is the mystery of deep worship.

Sure Mercies of David

Another type of covenant that exists between God and David is the *Sure Mercies of David*. This covenant is the mercy extended to any sinner who forsakes their old ways, and make a complete turnaround to the Lord. The *Sure Mercies of David* is released every time a sinner comes forward in repentance.

Elijah

Zealous Worshipper, Lone Prophet and Prayer Combatant

Notable Works:

Led Israel back to the worship of Yahweh

Mass slaughtered hundreds of prophets Jezebel's prophet

Shut Israel's heaven for 3 years, there was no rain

16

ELIJAH

KING DAVID'S DESIRE TO BUILD GOD'S HOUSE

> *Elijah stood in front of them and said, "How much longer will you try to have things both ways? If the LORD is God, worship him! But if Baal is God, worship him!" The people did not say a word.*
>
> **1 KING 18:21 NKJV**

The Elijah Assignment

It will only take worshippers to flip the entire world upside down. The fight of Elijah was the fight for Yahweh's Worship. Elijah's decree to shut down the rain supply was one decree to contend for worship. Elijah was a blatant worshipper. Elijah was tasked with reconciling the hearts of the lost children to the heart of the Father. His assignment was to search out adulterous children and bring them to worship the Lord. The Elijah mindset says "I am Yahweh's blatant worshipper! With powerful intensity I bow down only to Yahweh. My intention is bold and clear, nothing must get in the way to blur the identity of the Lord whom I worship".

When the entire nation goes the way of idolatry, when the

hearts of God's people are completely turned away when the altars of darkness are erected in the cities - the least desired message in the ears of the people is the call to worship. In the times of king Ahab, there was high resistance to worship Yahweh. In a time when the government of baal had occupied the hearts of the people, when the children of Israel had become hostile towards Yahweh, and were following closely in the steps of king Ahab - Prophet Elijah shows up as a one-man team member on the special mission of disrupting the worship of baal, tearing down baal's altars, and building Yahweh's altar.

Establishing Worship

In worship, there's a special mission requiring the establishment of Yahweh's worship altars in territories once occupied by darkness. Worshippers with this kind of assignments are required to use highly advanced spiritual weapons in order to succeed. The spirit of Elijah is needed to establish worship in areas that are fully charged with idolatry. Any worshipper who is sent to build worship altars must be spiritually charged to carry high voltage spiritual power before they can advance in their mission.

Instituting worship was Prophet Elijah's mission. A prophetic worship militant - Prophet Elijah is one who does undergoes warlike situations to establish worship altar of Yahweh. Elijah teaches an unconventional spiritual warfare in the mobilization of worship. He shuts down the supply of rain, suspended harvest of food supply thereby bringing hardship on the economy of Israel. Elijah declares, *"As the Lord lives, the God of Israel whom I serve, there will be no dew or rain except at my bidding"* - *1 Kings 17:1*. After his bold declaration, Israel experienced no rain, but country experience drought for 3 years. How did Elijah command so much authority over Israel? The most spiritually powerful and sensitive is given the power over a region. In this case, Elijah was the watchman over the region. The heavenly watchers assigned to Israel only waited for Elijah's decree and they obey. Every true worshipper is a watcher, standing in the spiritually highest place in their communities.

The War of Worship

Sending faminine into the land did not turn the hearts of the people back to the Lord in the times of Elijah. In places where there is infiltration of satanic prophets; people get really confused and defiant that it only takes the mercies of God to draw them into worship. Elijah said to the people:.

1 Kings 18:20-21 NKJV

"So Ahab sent for all the children of Israel, and gathered the prophets together on Mount Carmel. And Elijah came to all the people, and said, "How long will you falter between two opinions? If the Lord is God, follow Him; but if Baal, follow him." But the people answered him not a word."

Yahweh's side or Baal's side?

In one of our worship meetings, the Lord gave me a prophetic word to one of the women, the words were from Ecclesiastes 10:1 *Dead flies putrefy the perfumer's ointment, And cause it to give off a foul odor*; I asked the Lord what it meant, and the Lord said, tell her: STOP ALLOWING FLIES TO PERCH ON YOUR DESTINY.TELL HER TO STOP SEXUAL RELATIONS OUTSIDE OF MARRIAGE.

Afterwards, the Holy Spirit dropped the lyrics of a new song and the song had the lyrics of the verses quoted above, and special emphasis was draw on *"How long will you falter between two opinions? If the Lord is God, follow Him; but if Baal, follow him"*. During the worship, I knew whom the word was for, and after the worship session, God told me to release the words that was released earlier specifically to her. I met her where she was having a chat and she introduced herself as a minister who worked in the ministry of healing and

144

deliverance; God said to me; DELIVER THE MESSAGE AGAIN. So, I said to her, there was a word earlier for you, and God said: DEAD FLIES PUTREFY THE PERFUMER'S OINTMENT, AND CAUSE IT TO GIVE OFF FOUL ODOR. STOP ALLOWING FLIES TO PERCH ON YOUR DESTINY. THERE ARE MEN AROUND YOU THAT YOU ARE... She interrupted and said, "that word is absolutely on point, I understand it, you know, I come from a witchcraft background and...". This was someone whom the sick, the afflicted and those who needed the touch of the Lord would drop by a location where she was part of the lead healing ministers, she'll lay hands on them and leave people even worse off than they were originally. After hearing her story, we realized why God released the song lyrics, "If God be God or if Baal is". She left and never returned. Like this woman, there are thousands of thousands who mingle witchcraft and worship.

At Mount Carmel, Elijah began to ask the people, how long they would sit on the fence, just like Jesus said the lukewarm will be vomited out in Revelation 3:16. Elijah understood that the people would linger on in slavery and idolatry if the prophets of baal were left alone to continue.

1 Kings 18:22-24 NKJV

"Then Elijah said to the people, "I alone am left a prophet of the Lord; but Baal's prophets are four hundred and fifty men. Therefore let them give us two bulls; and let them choose one bull for themselves, cut it in pieces, and lay it on the wood, but put no fire under it; and I will prepare the other bull, and lay it on the wood, but put no fire under it. Then you call on the name of your gods, and I will call on the name of the Lord; and the God who answers by fire, He is God." So all the people answered and said, "It is well spoken"

Elijah needed to win the hearts of the people back to God, and He needed to do it quick. He had everything on the line, there were no backup plans. There were 450 men, plus the people who were all gathered heard when he made a case that his God was the One who answers by fire. This is the way of worship. A worshipper commits their entirety into God's hands, and does not forget to burn all the bridges of doubts off. This is the depth of faith is where the working power of God's unlimitedness comes to work.

Worship, Prophetic & Jezebel

Wherever worship is, there is prophetic revelation, and wherever the spirit of prophecy is, there is a spirit of Jezebel lurking around. Every worshipper must understand who Jezebel is and what Jezebel does and how she does it, otherwise the worshipper's ministry is ruined.

1 Kings 19:1-4 NKJV

"And Ahab told Jezebel all that Elijah had done, also how he had executed all the prophets with the sword. Then Jezebel sent a messenger to Elijah, saying, "So let the gods do to me, and more also, if I do not make your life as the life of one of them by tomorrow about this time." And when he saw that, he arose and ran for his life, and went to Beersheba, which belongs to Judah, and left his servant thereBut he himself went a day's journey into the wilderness, and came and sat down under a broom tree. And he prayed that he might die, and said, "It is enough! Now, Lord, take my life, for I am no better than my fathers!"

Who is Jezebel?

Jezebel is not a man or a woman. Jezebel is a spirit. The spirit of Jezebel had existed as far back as Adam and Eve existed. The spirit of Jezebel was the spirit at work in the life of Eve, although this spirit didn't go by the name Jezebel at the time. It was the spirit that took control and lured Adam out God's agenda and worship through obedience.

The manifestation of this spirit was seen clearly in the life of

Ahab's wife who was named queen Jezebel. More people became aware of this spirit from this time on. In the human sense, Jezebel was the wife of king Ahab of Israel.

Revelation 2:20 NKJV

" Nevertheless I have a few things against you, because you allow that woman Jezebel, who calls herself a prophetess, to teach and seduce My servants to commit sexual immorality and eat things sacrificed to idols"

God personally goes against any worshipper who gives room to the spirit of Jezebel. God become the rod of correction to any of His children who gives this spirit a chance. This spirit is good in harrassing worshipper out of God's presence with her demeanor and status. She seeks to hijack the truth of God, spread false teaching and lure God's servant into moral failure through sexual iniquities. Everyone God has called into worship must know the ways of Jezebel to overcome her complex and multiple schemes.

The Ways of Jezebel

The ways of Jezebel are many, the major ones are discussed below. The number 1 reason why many fall into the net of Jezebel is compromise on the word of God. Here are some ways Jezebel is ruining worship altars.

Way #1 Distracts from God's plan: When God calls a worshipper and gives the worshipper the mission and implementation plan of the assignment, Jezebel shows up to say words like, *"this is not the way or Senior pastor whom I worked with for 20 years used to do it. This is the way it should be done".* The worshipper seeks to lure the worshipper away from the agenda of God.

Way #2 Jezebel's Qualifications: Jezebel presents herself to appear as qualified. The spirit may claim to be a prophet or prophetess. Jezebel may have insights into the spirit realm, but Jezebel's access into the spirit realm is obtained from satanic means. Jezebel controls with anger, Jezebel controls with sexual intercourse. Jezebel presents herself as one who has a smooth relationship with God when nothing of such exists. Jezebel seeks to gain the trust of the people by appearing as godly, so she can spread her satanic motives. Jezebel says, *"If not for my prayers, you wouldn't have achieved this"*, *"my pastors cannot do without me, because I am the only prophet in the church who is so accurate"*, *"the church cannot function well without me because I coordinate multiple areas"*, *"your life cannot be the same if I cut you off."*. All these are red flags and the voices of Jezebel.

Way #3 Jezebel's Captives: Jezebel's captives are strong people with great missions from God. For Jezebel to succeed, they must have been careless or naive. Many of Jezebel's captives are ministers, pastors, prophets, evangelists. Jezebel gathers them all around her table. Jezebel has a collection of pastors and prophets whom is at her beck and call. *"Pastor, I need you to come to my house and worship with me, and bless me, I find it hard to sleep."*, *"Worship leader, I really cook good food, I can drop you food anytime you want"*. These are some of the voices of Jezebel and many ministers have been hooked to the chain of Jezebel because they succumbed to words like these.

Way #4 - Jezebel Occupies an Influential Position: Jezebel works her way to positions of authority. When she seeks to control the worshipper, she works her into the inner circle of the worshipper. In some cases, Jezebel becomes a spouse. In some cases, Jezebel becomes an assistant, a close confidant, a supporter, a donor, or a respected elder.

Way #5 - Jezebel's Mission: Jezebel fights is to pull down the godly leader or minister. In marriage situations, if the spirit of Jezebel is upon the wife, Jezebel seeks to derail her husband who is a worshipper. Jezebel may take up the image of a praying wife, one whom her husband is to place all worship and prayer related concerns upon because she can handle it all. Jezebel gently and slowly leads her away from the Lord. *"You are too spiritual"*, *"you are becoming a fanatic christian"*, *"there's nothing like spiritual warfare, stop deceiving yourself"*, *"You're taking this worship thing too seriously, I've been in the church 20 years and I know how it feels when people first convert"*. All these are Jezebel's tactic too lead the worshipper away from God.

Jezebel is not to be feared or exalted. She works in the depths of manipulation and only succeeds when her subject compromises. The worshipper's strongest weapon is worship. Worship comes with strong obedience to God and all His ways, with this tool, Jezebel has no chance.

Elijah & Prophetic Revelation

Elijah's encounter with God teaches vital lessons in prophetic revelation. He was a prophet, known to hear from God accurately. When God set a meeting with Elijah, the passage of God came through a wind, an earthquake, fire and a still small voice.

1 Kings 19:11-12 NKJV

" Then He said, "Go out, and stand on the mountain before the Lord." And behold, the Lord passed by, and a great and strong wind tore into the mountains and broke the rocks in pieces before the Lord, but the Lord was not in the wind; and after the wind an earthquake, but the Lord was not in the earthquake; and after the earthquake a fire, but the Lord was not in the fire; and after the fire a still small voice.

As a prophet who had witnessed God's move in fire, the flesh and natural mind could easily expect and limit the move of God through the channel of fire. We must never become familiar with God, because He is vast and beyond our understanding.

God chooses to speak to us in ways He want. The only way we would not miss God out on hearing from God is to remain open to all His ways.

Attributes of Elijah

Elijah was a zealous prophetic worshipper of God.Listed below are some of the traits of the great worshipper of God;

Attribute #1 - Accuracy of God's Word: God's word was accurate in the mouth of the prophet Elijah. God never allows the word of his true prophets to fall to the ground. God watches over those words and ensures it comes to pass. Worshippers like Elijah who worship the Lord with the entirety of their being are given constant access into God's decisions in heaven, and this brings about accuracy into the prophetic revelations given to them.

Attribute #2 - Confidence: Elijah had a high confidence in God. It is easy to claim to be on God's side when things seem fine and everyone seemed to be on the same side. What happens if we find out we are the only one left on God's side, would the same level of confidence be found in us?

Attribute #3 - Separated for God: Elijah was never afraid of being separated for God. He didn't go the way of others. He was set aside for God. Like Elijah, every fierce worshipper is called away from the distractions of life, and they are called into a life of walking with God

Attribute #4 - Difficult Times: Elijah was not exempted from the difficulties of life. One would have thought that despite the rare kind and working of God's power in the life of Elijah, there wouldn't be difficulty, there was, and an unexpected one. A man like Elijah fled at the threat of Jezebel, and even became suicidal.

Attribute #5 Difficult Times: Elijah was not exempted from the difficulties of life. One would have thought that despite the rare kind and working of God's power in the life of Elijah, there wouldn't be difficulty, there was, and an unexpected one. A man like Elijah fled at the threat of Jezebel, and even became suicidal.

Attribute #6 Less Human Supporters: Elijah had minimal human support. It is very common for worshippers to encounter this. The moment you become zealous for God, the less support you will get from humans. The children of God didn't only turn away from God, they tore down His altars, and hated Elijah that they sought to take his life for attempting to reconcile their hearts back to God.

Worshippers like Elijah are mandated to fight iniquity on a national scale. The Elijah worshippers when sent to leaders of nations never compromise on the word of God. They speak the pure truth. The Elijah worshippers are fierce worshippers. In spiritual battles, their victory stories are significant because they explore the most explosive weapons of fiery worship in warfare.

Daniel &

Friends

Uncompromising Worshippers, National Intercessor, filled with wisdom who took the name of Yahweh into the Babylonian government

Instituted:
The worship of Yahweh in the Babylonian government

Instituted:
The worship of Yahweh in the Babylonian government

Notable for

Translation of dreams

Defiant worshippers

Refusal to partake in the king's delicacies
Understanding of the times and season appointed for Israel's deliverance
Readiness to give up their life rather than to worship another god
Unhurt in the fiery furnace

17

DANIEL, HANAIAH, MISAHEL & AZARIAH

REFUSAL OF THE KING'S DELICACIES

> "But Daniel purposed in his heart that he would not defile himself with the portion of the king's delicacies, nor with the wine which he drank; therefore he requested of the chief of the eunuchs that he might not defile himself."
>
> **DANIEL 1:8 NKJV**

Some worshippers are given the burden for nations, Daniel was one of those worshippers. Separated, undefiled and well-read, Daniel's life of worship is a perfect study for both young and adult worshippers, prophets, students, scholars, intercessors, christian politicians, community leaders and everyone who desires to learn the ways of worship. A careful study of Daniel's life will clarify that worshippers are not exempted from tests and seasons of trials in life. A study of Daniel's life also gives us a closer look into the lifestyle of the worshipper in lowly times and in prosperous times.

The study in this chapter combines the study of Daniel's life with the study of the life of his three Hebrew friends; Hanaiah, Mishael and Azariah because their worship stories are intertwined. In captivity, these worshippers were not tested as silver, but they were tested as golden vessels in the furnace of affliction - and they came out gloriously by the power of the Lord.

THE ANOINTED FOUR IN THE KING'S COURT

Nebuchadnezzar king of Babylon had taken Jerusalem into slavery, and the four worshippers - Daniel, Hananiah, Misahel and Azariah were amongst those taken into captivity.

Daniel 1:3-6 NKJV

"Then the king instructed Ashpenaz, the master of his eunuchs, to bring some of the children of Israel and some of the king's descendants and some of the nobles, young men in whom there was no blemish, but good-looking, gifted in all wisdom, possessing knowledge and quick to understand, who had ability to serve in the king's palace, and whom they might teach the language and literature of the Chaldeans. And the king appointed for them a daily provision of the king's delicacies and of the wine which he drank, and three years of training for them, so that at the end of that time they might serve before the king. Now from among those of the sons of Judah were Daniel, Hananiah, Mishael, and

Azariah. To them the chief of the eunuchs gave names: he gave Daniel the name Belteshazzar; to Hananiah, Shadrach; to Mishael, Meshach; and to Azariah, Abed-Nego."

In slavery, the kings called for a separation of the best amongst the slaves and the four worshippers made the selection. It was not by chance. Why were the four worshippers selected? THE ANOINTING OF GOD.

What is the Anointing Oil of God?
The anointing of oil of God is a representation of the Holy Spirit and power of God. One of the functions of the anointing oil is to make the anointed become hallowed. The anointing creates a demarcation around the glory of God in the life of the anointed, and the carrier of the anointing becomes separated and consecrated for God. Wherever the anointed goes, they become separated.

War Against the Anointed Worshipper
Every anointed worshipper is warred against. Daniel's name means YAHWEH IS MY JUDGE. Hananiah means YAHWEH IS GLORIOUS. Mishael means WHO IS LIKE THE MIGHTY ONE. Azariah means YAHWEH HAS HELPED. A major part of a person's essence is in their name. With a person's name, God can be worshipped, and with a person's name, an idol can be worshipped. A person's name beckons to either God or the devil. A person's name originates from God or from the devil. Knowing the outstanding power in a name, the king of Babylon changed the worshippers names as follows; Daniel to Belteshazzar to Hananiah to Shadrach, Mishael to Meshach; and from Azariah to Abed-Nego. The original names of the worshippers were in alignment with God. The king, after choosing them as the best amongst their peers, changed their name to names associated with his gods. The name change was the first attack on their faith designed to silence their worship. The men were not deterred.

FASTING & WORSHIP

Daniel and his friends chose to stay away from fancy food and fine wine - worshipping God through their choice of food. That too, is a kind of fasting.

Daniel 1:8-10 & 12-20 NKJV

"But Daniel purposed in his heart that he would not defile himself with the portion of the king's delicacies, nor with the wine which he drank; therefore he requested of the chief of the eunuchs that he might not defile himself. Now God had brought Daniel into the favor and goodwill of the chief of the eunuchs. ....Please test your servants for ten days, and let them give us vegetables to eat and water to drink. Then let our appearance be examined before you, and the appearance of the young men who eat the portion of the king's delicacies; and as you see fit, so deal with your servants." So he consented with them in this matter, and tested them ten days. And at the end of ten days their features appeared better and fatter in flesh than all the young men who ate the portion of the king's delicacies. Thus the steward took away their portion of delicacies and the wine that they were to drink, and gave them vegetables. As for these four young men, God gave them knowledge and skill in all literature and wisdom; and Daniel had understanding in all visions and dreams. Now at the end of the days, when the king had said that they should be brought in, the chief of the eunuchs brought them in before Nebuchadnezzar. Then the king interviewed them, and among them all none was found like Daniel, Hananiah, Mishael, and Azariah; therefore they served before the king. And in all matters of wisdom and understanding about which the king examined them, he found them ten times better than all the magicians and astrologers who were in all his realm."

The Worshipper & Fasting

Fasting is the affliction of the soul. Fasting keeps defilement out of the soul. Fasting keeps the flesh under subjection. Fasting brings the soul into a deeper connection with the Lord. In fasting, the soul of the worshipper open to the power and effectiveness of God's Holy Spirit; and in communion with the mind of God. A soul who is connected to the Lord receives all types of godly wisdom and visions. Likewise, a soul connected to satan taps from satanic wisdom. In Daniel, Hanainaiah, Mishael and Azariah's cases, the four were connected to the wisdom of God as their souls were undefiled that their wisdom were 10x better than what was found in the magicians.

With Daniel and the three, it was no doubt that their sacrifice of fasting from the king's fine food and wine was accepted by the Lord and their harvest was an outpouring of rare knowledge, skills and wisdom. Knowing their bodies were temples of God, they refused to be defiled by the king's food, and they came a repository of God's wisdom.

God wants to give access into heavenly wisdom, He wants to give results of heaven's decisions and plans. He also wants to give access to worshippers who would influence the decisions of heaven through prayers, but He will only give to the worshipper. Daniel was an example of a worshipper who received access into Heaven's wisdom. He received an abundance of wisdom through worship, fasting and prayers.

DREAMS, VISIONS & REVELATIONS

Dream

What is a dream? Dream is a way through which God communicates information to us. We cannot see God with our physical eyes, hence, God speaks to people through God. Dreams takes place in the soul of man. There are varying levels of the gifts of dreams. Dreams are one of the most secured ways God speaks to people. God is highly confidential, yet He seeks to reveal information that will help people live lives triumphantly. There are information that are very sensitive, requiring only the attention of the recipient of the information, in this case, the dreamer. This is why God does not reveal clear information to people when they seek prophecy. God may find them careless with information. He may choose to hide information for the benefits of the hearer, sometimes because the hearer is not spiritually mature or the fullness of time for such revelation has not occurred. This is why God gives dreams in proverbs.

Some people are given revelation through frequent dreams. For some, the dream is their primary mode of receiving information from God. For some, they are able to translate the dreams of others. God has also gifted some people to be able to translate the dreams of others without receiving details of the information from the dream. Daniel was blessed with such a rare gift.

Dreams are so powerful that satanic diviners cannot translate dreams if dreams are not explained to them. Believers need to learn how to ask God for the translation of their dreams. If dreams are revealed to those who are not working under the power of the Holy Spirit, there are some dangers to that. One of those dangers is that they have the information about a person's life that can be used for evil. Second, they may not understand and prophesy evil. Third, the Spirit of God confuses them, and the dreamer begins to work on the wrong information. Only God's spirit can translate dreams accurately. The worshipper can request the gifts of dream translation.

Prayers of Daniel

Blessed be the name of God forever and ever, Wisdom and might are yours. You change the times and the seasons; You remove kings and raises up kings; You give wisdom to the wise. And knowledge to those who have understanding. You reveals deep and secret things; You knows what *is* in the darkness, And light dwells with you. Shower me with your wisdom and might

Attempt to Mock Worship

Worship is sacred. The devil seeks to mock worship. The devil seeks to turn worship into entertainment unto himself. In captivity, the devil demanded through the Babylonians that the Israelites sing one of their worship songs, seeking to mock them. Knowing how sacred the worship of Yahweh is, the enslaved Israelites refused and the Scripture below captures the story:

Psalm 137:1-9

Beside the rivers of Babylon, we sat and wept as we thought of Jerusalem. We put away our harps, hanging them on the branches of poplar trees. For our captors demanded a song from us. Our tormentors insisted on a joyful hymn". "Sing us one of those songs of Jerusalem!" But how can we sing the songs of the Lord while in a pagan land?If I forget you, O Jerusalem, let my right hand forget how to play the harp. May my tongue stick to the roof of my mouth if I fail to remember you, if I don't make Jerusalem my greatest joy. O Lord, remember what the Edomites did on the day the armies of Babylon captured Jerusalem. "Destroy it!" they yelled. "Level it to the ground!" O Babylon, you will be destroyed. Happy is the one who pays you back for what you have done to us. Happy is the one who takes your babies and smashes them against the rocks!

A new version of the Babylonian riverside experience is playing out in worship gatherings where jokes and comedy is brought into the house of God for entertainment. Many comedians coming to play in church use the same songs birthed by the Holy Spirit to worship Yahweh, and change to their comedy theme to provide amusement to the people, thereby perverting worship. There is no difference between the demand of the Babylonian captors and gatherings where comedy and entertainment is used to amuse the people. The Babylonians had heard about the worship of Yahweh. Wanting to derive pleasure, they sought to toy with sacred songs and asked that their Israelites captives sing the songs of Yahweh to them, but God's people refused. Similarly, any comedy designed for Church so that the congregation to laugh is a form of idol worship. It is designed to derive pleasure for the originator which often times is the devil.

The three Hebrew kids had the revelation of true worship that they could easily discern false worship. They were worshippers of the Living God and they could easily identify false worship. Nebuchadnezzar wanting to receive worship for the statue he had created called for mass worship. When the stage of false worship was set. The entire Babylon was called to worship, all types of instruments were to be used. The entity to be worshipped was a statue and the children of covenant purposed in their hearts "whether you decorate the stage or not, you may sing your songs sweetly and add fancy lights to it, we will not bow because that is not the worship of YHWH". The Hebrew kids understood the covenant of worship they had made with God, and they answered the king:

Daniel 3:16-18 NKJV

"Shadrach, Meshach, and Abed-Nego answered and said to the king, "O Nebuchadnezzar, we have no need to answer you in this matter. If that is the case, our God whom we serve is able to deliver us from the burning fiery furnace, and He will deliver us from your hand, O king. But if not, let it be known to you, O king, that we do not serve your gods, nor will we worship the gold image which you have set up."

The Battle For Worship: 3 Hebrew Worshippers

Every worshipper fights in this war. For the three Hebrew Worshippers, the choice was set before them; worship the image created by the king Nebuchadnezzer or be thrown into the fire. Getting thrown into the fire meant that the worshippers would not compromise by bowing to any other gods, but Yahweh. They chose the hard way out. The spirit of Nebucadnezzer still lives, and this spirit demands worship from the worshipper. Most times, the spirit of Nebuchadnezzar is positioned in a place of influence in the worshipper's life. At the appointed time, Nebuchadnezzar begins to demand worship. The spirit of Nebuchadnezzar manifests in many ways; the worshipper finds a job and worship becomes a burden. It is the spirit of Nebuchadnezzar at work whenever any choice of whether to go into worship of God, or pay attention to something else.

When this spirit is at work, there are only two things that can happen. The first is that the worshipper refuses to yield and choose the way of God. It may not look like the easiest thing to do, in fact it will not look, it may come as another version of the fiery furnace experience, but God will definitely be glorified. The second possibility is for a person to go in the way of the false worship. It is always the easy way out, and unfortunately, many people take this way, but the end is doom.

The Battle For Worship: Daniel

Every worshipper fights in this war. For the three Hebrew Worshippers, the choice was set before them; worship the image created by the king Nebuchadnezzer or be thrown into the fire. Getting thrown into the fire meant that the worshippers would not compromise by bowing to any other gods, but Yahweh. They chose the hard way out. The spirit of Nebucadnezzer still lives, and this spirit demands worship from the worshipper. Most times, the spirit of Nebuchadnezzar is positioned in a place of influence in the worshipper's life. At the appointed time, Nebuchadnezzar begins to demand worship. The spirit of Nebuchadnezzar manifests in many ways; the worshipper finds a job and worship becomes a burden. It is the spirit of Nebuchadnezzar at work whenever any choice of whether to go into worship of God, or pay attention to something else.

When this spirit is at work, there are only two things that can happen. The first is that the worshipper refuses to yield and choose the way of God. It may not look like the easiest thing to do, in fact it will not look, it may come as another version of the fiery furnace experience, but God will definitely be glorified. The second possibility is for a person to go in the way of the false worship. It is always the easy way out, and unfortunately, many people take this way, but the end is doom.

Attributes of Daniel

Attribute #1 - A Man of Prayer: Daniel constantly lived in prayers. Daniel 6: 10 records, *"Now when Daniel knew that the writing was signed, he went home. And in his upper room, with his windows open toward Jerusalem, he knelt down on his knees three times that day, and prayed and gave thanks before his God, as was his custom since early days".* even when the law of the land says otherwise.

Attribute #2 - Eating Habits: Daniel abstained from choice food to keep his body sanctified for God. He worshipped God with fasting. A worshipper must not allow their belly to be their god.

Attribute #3 - Reader: Daniel was a reader. Daniel's reading lifestyle gave him insights into history and the deliverance of Israel. He was quoted saying, "I Daniel understood by books" in Daniel 9:2.

Attribute #4 - Journal The revelation of God's knowledge, power and glory is costly. A worshipper understands that and keeps a journal.

Attribute #5 - Excellence A community is compared excellence where their works are not comparable to others in terms of goodness. When other countries - excellence that is found in the life of an individual - like the same kind of excellence you found in the life of Daniel. When people were enslaved from Jerusalem to Babylon. He knew that the worshippers of YHWH have insight. He chose them to serve in his palace. Teach them languages in the space of 3 years. The Nebuchadnezzar interview.. People who should be in a position of leadership and decision making. They were able to learn a difficult language in the space of 3 years. . The king interviewed them in different aspects, in the field of astrology - the study of stars, the study of heavenly bodies.. They understood literature, they had the skill.

Attribute #6 - Right Associations A worshipper's association impacts the worshipper's lifestyle. Daniel understood this, and the only people the Scripture records as Daniel's friend were the three hebrew worshippers. A worshipper cannot associate with those whose God is not Yahweh.

Attribute #7 - **Angelic Visitations** Daniel had angelic visitations. From Daniel's life, we learn of angel Gabriel's role, as a communication ministering angel of God.

Attribute #8 - **National Intercessor** Daniel took upon the burden of the national and prayed unto the Lord. *"Now while I was speaking, praying, and confessing my sin and the sin of my people Israel, and presenting my supplication before the Lord my God for the holy mountain of my God, yes, while I was speaking in prayer, the man Gabriel, whom I had seen in the vision at the beginning, being caused to fly swiftly, reached me about the time of the evening offering. And he informed me, and talked with me, and said, "O Daniel, I have now come forth to give you skill to understand"* - Daniel 9:20-22

The Samaritan Woman

The Inquisitive Woman with an Uncolorful Past and a Fragmented Life who Became an Evangelist

Notable for

Curious about worship

18

THE SAMARITAN WOMAN

A broken life is all I have got, I give it to you. Take it all for your glory. This is the attitude of the woman with the broken life who became the first evangelist.

Jesus said to her, "Go, call your husband, and come here."The woman answered and said, "I have no husband." Jesus said to her, "You have well said, 'I have no husband,' for you have had five husbands, and the one whom you now have is not your husband; in that you spoke truly. The woman said to Him, "Sir, I perceive that You are a prophet. Our fathers worshiped on this mountain, and you Jews say that in Jerusalem is the place where one ought to worship."

JOHN 4:20 NKJV

A woman who's gone through five marriage must have gone through different forms emotional pains. In all the marriages she had gone through, she had gone through a lot. She probably had met a lot of accusations in her journey and she wasn't expecting less from Jesus. She was ready for another wave of accusation. So on the day she met Jesus, she was ready, in a defensive posture, waiting for another accusation. The moment she realized that she had just found someone who was ready to give her something for the first time in her life, the living water, the tone in her voice changed. When the word of life came into her, she became a woman evangelist. She evangelized the entire town. She also turned them to disciples, because she took them to where Jesus is. For them to follow her, she must have been really convincing.

Humility and repentance is one of the ways to heaven. That's why the uncircumsized mind does not understand forgiveness and repentance. The uncircumcised mind does not understand mercy in judgement. The uncircumsized mind does not love. One of the hidden mystery in worship is humility. The mystery of worship cannot be unveiled in a lifetime; and that is why God is birthing so many prophetic worshippers, worshipper who are given insights and foresights into the processes of heaven, into the secrets of ages to come, that they might let the world know that man's all is worship.

Breaking the Barriers to Worship

Attribute #1 - Total Repentance Daniel constantly lived in prayers. Daniel 6: 10 records, *"Now when Daniel knew that the writing was signed, he went home. And in his upper room, with his windows open toward Jerusalem, he knelt down on his knees three times that day, and prayed and gave thanks before his God, as was his custom since early days".* even when the law of the land says otherwise.

Attribute #2 - Humility: Daniel abstained from choice food to keep his body sanctified for God. He worshipped God with fasting. A worshipper must not allow their belly to be their god.

Attribute #3 – **Faith:** Daniel was a reader. Daniel's reading lifestyle gave him insights into history and the deliverance of Israel. He was quoted saying, "I Daniel understood by books" in Daniel 9:2.

Woman With the Jar of Perfume

The worshipper who gave more than her 1/10th, but all her year's wage to prepare Jesus for His burial

Notable for

Purchasing a jar of perfume with her entire year's earnings for the anointing of Jesus.

19

THE WOMAN WITH THE JAR OF PERFUME

Worship is costly. Worship comes at a price. When the carnal mind sees the extravagance of worship; they only have one thing to say, and that is "what waste is this ?". This unnamed woman was a sinner who met with her Savior. She was already working in revelation with powerful insight. She knew the time of Jesus' death was near, right under the nose of the disciples, she anointed Jesus ahead of his burial. Pouring her flask of oil upon Jesus was a prophetic reoccurrence of what happened 33 years ago when the wise men brought myrrh (a major ingredient used as part of the mixture spices for the dead) to Jesus at his birth.

Matthew 26:7-11 NKJV

"And when Jesus was in Bethany at the house of Simon the leper, a woman came to Him having an alabaster flask of very costly fragrant oil, and she poured it on His head as He sat at the table. But when His disciples saw it, they were indignant, saying, "Why this waste? For this fragrant oil might have been sold for much and given to the poor." But when Jesus was aware of it, He said to them, "Why do you trouble the woman? For she has done a good work for Me. For you have the poor with you always, but Me you do not have always. For in pouring this fragrant oil on My body, she did it for My burial. Assuredly, I say to you, wherever this gospel is preached in the whole world, what this woman has done will also be told as a memorial to her."

Jesus accounted the costly worship to good works and itThis woman was working in deep revelation with powerful foresight - repeating what had happened 33 years ago when the wise men brought myrrh as part of gifts.The jar of perfume she poured upon the feet of Jesus was estimated to worth a yearly income.

Worship & The Leadership of the Holy Spirit
No two worship sessions is the same. We can worship God through all that we do, in words, thoughts, deeds, songs, acts of kindness, dance, music, giving - all that we do. Each time we worship, the Holy Spirit leads us. The Spirit led that woman to anoint Jesus. That was the type of worship the Lord wanted from her at the moment. The disciples were thinking she could have spent her money in charity. Worship is never to be approached by the human mind.

Left to the disciples, they would have orchestrated a different type of worship, and advised the woman on the way to worship God. But God's plans and purpose was different from theirs.

The Second Anointing of Jesus

Jesus was anointed only twice when he was on earth. The first anointing came directly from God. The second anointing came from where no one expected - the former sinful woman.

The mission of Jesus was the most expensive worship mission on earth - to die for the sins of the world, even for those yet unborn. So was the perfume purchased for the anointing preceding his death; the perfume was estimated to be a year's worth of the woman's earnings. It was the plan of God, not of man, also for the anointing of the Savior-to-be come from the forsaken woman whose former sinful ways was in the public knowledge.

The Anointing for Empowerment of the Death of Jesus

One of the functions of the anointing is to make the anointed become hallowed. The anointing creates a demarcation around the life of a person. The anointing creates a barricade of the purpose of God around the carrier. The anointing also carries the power of God, and it can function as a channel of God's power into a person's life to empower a mission. The anointing was the anointing for empowerment.

The woman with the jar of oil caught the revelation, she didn't hold back, and she became the only person that was given the grace to anoint Jesus Christ. A privilege like no other! She anointed Jesus for the empowerment to be able to fulfill His mission - carrying the cross and sins of the world, and dying a gruesome death in isolation, rejection, shame - even as His Father takes His eyes off Him. The anointing of Jesus by God through the woman marked the beginning of the sufferings that the Messiah went through. Jesus came as a man, and He had to be anointed for empowerment to carry all the sufferings, otherwise, He would have backed out.

Why The Woman With the Jar of Spikenard Oil?

Why was the woman the one to carry out the anointing ministry?. There were many who had been with Jesus. Those whom He had taught the ways of the Kingdom of God. Those whom were no stranger to His parables, and had encountered the manifestations of his healing and deliverance ministry, those who He had taught the lessons of prayers, and has called into His inner circle. But He chose to use the worship from the woman the world saw as a sinner to confound the wise.

Luke 6:41-48 NKJV

"There was a certain creditor who had two debtors. One owed five hundred denarii, and the other fifty. And when they had nothing with which to repay, he freely forgave them both. Tell Me, therefore, which of them will love him more?" Simon answered and said, "I suppose the one whom he forgave more." And He said to him, "You have rightly judged." Then He turned to the woman and said to Simon, "Do you see this woman? I entered your house; you gave Me no water for My feet, but she has washed My feet with her tears and wiped them with the hair of her head. You gave Me no kiss, but this woman has not ceased to kiss My feet since the time I came in. You did not anoint My head with oil, but this woman has anointed My feet with fragrant oil. Therefore I say to you, her sins, which are many, are forgiven, for she loved much. But to whom little is forgiven, the same loves little." Then He said to her, "Your sins are forgiven."

We may never know the reason why God chose the woman, but there are lessons to be drawn from her worship:.

Lesson #1 - Contriteness & Brokenness of Heart- God is love, and we got the emotion of love from Him. God loves deeply and widely across the farthest lengths, breadths, widths and heights that we would ever be able to comprehend as humans. The tears of a worshipper is precious to God, so precious that He stores in a bottle, Psalm 56:8 says: *You number my wanderings; Put my tears into Your bottle; Are they not in Your book?* The woman was heartbroken, that Jesus said concerning the tears in her face: *"she has washed My feet with her tears".*

Lesson #2 - No Validation From Humans A worshipper must not seek the validation of men to continue in worship. If you've lived a sinful life, and have met with salvation of the Lord, you must not be seeking the approval of humans as a confirmation for your acceptable worship.

Lesson #3 - Humility: The spirit of humility was upon her. The image portrayed by Scripture is one of humility and reverence. The Lord dwells in the place of humility, and

20

THE 3 WISE MEN

THE WISE MEN FROM THE EAST WORSHIP JESUS`
Now after Jesus was born in Bethlehem of Judaea in the days of Herod the king, behold, wise men from the East came to Jerusalem, saying, "where is He who has been born King of the Jews? For we have seen His star in the East and have come to worship Him"

MATTHEW 2:1

The wise men were the observers of times. All the way from the East, the observers of times and seasons trailed the star of Jesus to Bethlehem. These men travelled far from their homelands and countries looking and following the direction and leading of wisdom and prophecy into Bethlehem. The wise men understood what privileges they were given to have lived at a time that Jesus was born. Having seen the start of Jesus, they got on their way and headed out on a journey to worship Jesus. People rarely set out on a journey without it costing them anything. When they located Jesus, they fell down to worship the baby Jesus. *The three wise men had to travel all the way from Asia being led by the* star. For the wise men, it was an expensive journey. From the moment the child was born until 2 years after. It was not this present day you could buy a plane ticket and fly there for the few hours. They travelled by camel, not horse. They came to bow for the king of kings.

The content of their gifts - they brought gold, talking about royalty, they came to pay homage to the King of kings.

Matthew 21:11

And when they had come into the house, they saw the young Child with Mary His mother, and fell down and worshipped Him. And when they had opened their treasures, they presented gifts to Him: gold, frankincense and myrrh.

There is great significance in the worship of the wise men. Following their worship was presentation of gifts to Jesus. Their choice of gifts were spiritually symbolic and prophetic. Their gifts represented who Jesus is, His assignment no earth and the things to come.

Gold: They presented Him with gold; a symbol of His royal status as the Son of God and the King He is to become and the Kingdom to be given to Him.

Frankincense: A symbol of His assignment on earth; symbolizing intercession and the representation of the aroma of Christ, the Word of God, soon to be released to the masses. In the book of Revelation; the scripture tells us the spiritual meaning of incense as the prayers of the saints.

And the twenty-four elders of the heavenly Sanhedrin] prostrated themselves before the Lamb. Each was holding a harp (lute or guitar), and they had golden bowls full of incense (fragrant spices and gums for burning), which are the prayers of God's people (the saints).

177

Part of His mission on earth was to open up a new way for us to pray directly to the Father using His name. *Jesus said to him, "I am the way, the truth, and the life. No one comes to the Father except through Me"* - John 14:6

Myrrh: In the Jewish culture, myrrh part of the spices used in the anointing of the dead. Mary, the mother of Jesus would have wondered why people coming to visit her baby bring an item that was used in anointing the dead. The wise men, having been given insight, brought myrrh as a representation of what is to come, preparing Him for the sacrifice and death that is to come about 32 years later.

Apostle Paul

The former persecutor of Christians who encountered Jesus and became a church planter.

Instituted:

Planted and strengthened the church

Notable for

Writing many books of the New Testament.

21

APOSTLE PAUL

APOSTLE PAUL TAUGHT WORSHIP AS A LIFESTYLE

"Therefore, I urge you, brothers and sisters, in view of God's mercy, to offer your bodies as a living sacrifice, holy and pleasing to God—this is your true and proper worship"

ROMANS 12:1

Apostle Paul's teachings focused on how Christians can introduce worship to every segment of their lives. The Book of Romans was the writing of Apostle Paul. Apostle Paul had the revelation of worship as a lifestyle. He had the revelation of the body as the sanctuary of God. Apostle Paul said in Romans 12:1 *"Therefore, I urge you, brothers and sisters, in view of God's mercy, to offer your bodies as a living sacrifice, holy and pleasing to God—this is your true and proper worship"*. This verse tells the worshiper - your body is sacred, with consecrated living, you can offer your body to God and the Lord counts it as worship unto Him. Apostle Paul's teachings of worship were majorly on the Christian living.

Apostle Paul's had revelations in majority of all areas of Christian living. He was given revelation on faith, salvation, grace, spiritual gifts and many areas of the Christian life. Apostle Paul was one of the few people who had the longest writings in the Scriptures, and this was through His relationship with the Holy Spirit. One of Apostle Paul's teachings is on the subject of grace. Every worshipper must understand grace for it is; and not how satan has marketed grace in the current times.

Grace As It In Heaven

The mystery of the kingdom of God has been released to the worshipper; and for this reason, a worshipper never takes the spirit of grace for granted. A worshipper understands the cost of grace and does not squander grace. Today, there are many false teachers, spreading a strange type of grace, there are many who come to the altar almost naked to minister, many who still engage in acts that defy the word of God, and claim they're covered by grace.

Grace only abides in the presence of God. Understanding grace from God's perspectives helps the worshipper stay away from the pitfalls of false grace.

General Grace: The only type of grace given freely is the grace for salvation. There is a special type of grace received by everyone who acknowledges Jesus, the Son of the Living God as their Lord and Savior. Without the grace for salvation, a sinner will hear the gospel and they will never understand. Without this type of grace, the mind of the sinner is veiled and no revelation or light of the gospel will ever shine into their hearts. However, a person who has received the grace for salvation is cut to their hearts when they hear the gospel and they make a decision. The only grace available for a sinner is the grace to receive salvation; just as the only prayer of a sinner that is answered is the prayer of repentance. After getting saved; there is general grace available for every new believer. "*For by grace you have been saved through faith, and that not of yourselves; it is the gift of God* - Ephesians 2:8. General Grace is the grace that is available and obtained at the time of salvation. Grace is a form of gift. You can give a gift to someone, and they collect it and never use it. And you can give a gift to another person and they make a really good use of the gift. Same can be said about the grace of God. At the time of salvation, a kind of grace called "General Grace" is given to the new believer. It is the grace that covers the former sins. The grace that places the new believer in a place of safety and exemption from the repayment of sins. All the vacuum is the life of the new believer is filled at the time of receiving salvation under the general grace.

Specific Grace: There is another category of grace. It is also called grace for specificity. It is a deeper form of grace that goes beyond salvation deeper grace beyond salvation. Specific grace is the kind of grace needed for specific missions in life. needed. The specific grace is also called "the *grace of life*". The grace of life is the specific grace needed to fulfill specific assignments in life. This type of grace is not like the general grace. It is not given until it is sought. It is not given to everyone, it is given to only those who diligently seek it. It is not a grace that can be obtained by being called a "church-goer"; It is the grace obtained through deep worship.

The specific grace is only released unto individuals who have accepted the general grace and also proven to be good stewards of the measure of general grace given to them. The grace of specificity is for specific assignments like leadership, parenting, marriage, career and more. The specific grace is obtained by those who are able to go into the presence of the Father: "*Let us therefore come boldly to the throne of grace, that we may obtain mercy and find grace to help in time of need*" - Hebrews 4:16. Considering that there is a high level of holiness required as stated in Hebrews 12:14 - *Make every effort to live in peace with everyone and to be holy; without holiness no one will see the Lord.* Without holiness, a worshipper worships in vain. Only those who go to the Father in holiness, humility and contriteness of heart will be able to access his presence and receive the grace needed for life. Here is why only deep worshippers are given special grace than the general population, because, a worshipper does not abuse the spirit of grace.

MAJOR REVELATIONS GIVEN TO APOSTLE PAUL

Revelation #1 - Speaking In Tongues

One of the secrets behind Apostle Paul effectiveness in ministry is that he spoke in tongues a lot. *I thank God that I speak in tongues more than all of you* - 1 Corinthians 14:18. Although today, many fancy churches today have barred their congregants for speaking in tongues. The role of speaking in tongues in the worshipper's life is significant. A worshipper who speaks in tongues gets effectiveness, power and clarity; because they commune with the Father, they pray the heart of the Father. One of the ways the devil tries to pervert speaking in tongues is to either discredit it or false break into tongues. A worshipper who speaks in tongues travels fast in worship.

Revelation #2 - Revelation of the Spiritual Gifts

The spiritual realm is an enormous world on its own. It is vast, the human mind cannot comprehend. Many are not aware of the existence of this world even though we have an existence in it. In the spiritual world, most physical rules we know about does not apply. Spiritually, there are cultures of different types, creatures of different tribes, and a lot of rules that doesn't make sense when weighed on the scales of logic. Apostle Paul received the revelations of spiritual gifts.

1 Corinthians 12:4-11 NKJV

There are diversities of gifts, but the same Spirit. There are differences of ministries, but the same Lord. And there are diversities of activities, but it is the same God who works all in all. But the manifestation of the Spirit is given to each one for the profit of all: for to one is given the word of wisdom through the Spirit, to another the word of knowledge through the same Spirit, to another faith by the same Spirit, to another gifts of healings by the same Spirit, to another the working of miracles, to another prophecy, to another discerning of spirits, to another different kinds of tongues, to another the interpretation of tongues. But one and the same Spirit works all these things, distributing to each one individually as He wills.

Revelation #3 - Spiritual War

The Apostle also received the revelation on spiritual war, helping the believer under that each of put together

Revelation #4 - Church Planting & Administration

Apostle Paul also received revelations on Church planting. He taught about how the members of the body of Christ are given different giftings for the building up of the church.

1 Corinthians 12:27-28NKJV

Now you are the body of Christ, and members individually. And God has appointed these in the church: first apostles, second prophets, third teachers, after that miracles, then gifts of healings, helps, administrations, varieties of tongues.

From the above verses, the building up of the body of Christ requires

John

The witness who walked in the power of Elijah but performed no miracle, sticking to his purpose

Notable for
Making way for the coming of the Lord

22

JOHN

THE FAITHFUL WITNESS

"And he will turn many of the children of Israel to the Lord their God. he will also go before Him in the spirit and power of Elijah, to turn the hearts of the fathers to the children, and the disobedient to the wisdom of the past, to make ready a people prepared for the Lord". Like 1:17

LUKE 1:17 NKJV

The ministry of John the Baptist is a rare one. The world was not ready for the Messiah, John was sent as a forerunner to prepare the way. John was sent ahead of Jesus to prepare for the entrance of the gospel.. His role was to get people ready for the message of Jesus and to reconcile the hearts of the people back to the Father. As simple as that may sound, it was a tough ministry, because even John didn't know whom the Messiah was, yet he bore witness of the Messiah. Such faith. John was called to give testimony about the Light, so that when the Light comes, people would believe. That light was Jesus, however John also didn't know who he was.

John 1:6-8

There was a man sent from God, whose name was John. This man came for a witness to bear witness of the Light, that all through him might believe. He was not the Light, but was sent to bear witness to that Light.

Ministry Without Miracles Staying in His purpose

John understood his purpose, he stayed with the mission and did not deviate from him. John had the spirit and power of Elijah upon his life - that means he could call fire down from heaven, he could order the rain not to fall, but He did not. But he did not work outside his purpose. He spent his entire ministry preparing the way for the Lord. John performed no signs and wonders throughout his ministry.

John 10:41

Then many came to Him and said, "John performed no sign, but all the things that John spoke about this man were true."`

Refused To Take God's Glory

John carried on with baptizing in water. He kept on doing what he was called to do, to baptize into repentance. He kept baptizing awaiting the Messiah, not knowing who He was or when He was going to show up.

John 1:29-34

The next day John saw Jesus coming toward him, and said, "Behold! The Lamb of God who takes away the sin of the world! This is He of whom I said, 'After me comes a Man who is preferred before me, for He was before me.' I did not know Him; but that He should be revealed to Israel, therefore I came baptizing with water." And John bore witness, saying, "I saw the Spirit descending from heaven like a dove, and He remained upon Him. I did not know Him, but He who sent me to baptize with water said to me, 'Upon whom you see the Spirit descending, and remaining on Him, this is He who baptizes with the Holy Spirit.' And I have seen and testified that this is the Son of God.

John's Humility: Lesson for the Worshipper

Lucifer stopped allowing worship to flow through him wanted worship to flow to him directly. Jesus is the Light, but many prefer to be the Light today. Many do not want to be the witness of Light. It can be so tempting when God begins to use us for His work to want to get out of our roles and become that Light. The enemy tries hard to push worshippers into the depths of pride. Every worshipper must understand that we are all human and must put our flesh under constant subjection. Like John, the worshipper must not leave their purpose, and run far away from jealousy, envy or competition.

John 1:35-37:1

Again, the next day, John stood with two of his disciples. And looking at Jesus as He walked, he said, "Behold the Lamb of God!". The two disciples heard him speak and they followed Jesus

When Jesus began his ministry, Jesus' first disciples were the disciples of John. When the two disciples heard and recognized what John had been preparing them for, they knew that it was time to be reconnected back to the Light. John did not become upset that his disciples went with Jesus. In fact, it was a moment of success for his ministry.

Considering John's prophetic anointing, he had the power to do things Elijah did, he did not use his power in the way Elijah did. He used the power to baptize people unto repentance and prepare them to receive the Lord. In whatever capacity you are spreading the gospel, the power of the Holy Spirit is needed for you to accomplish that mission. It is also important to catch the vision and hold onto what we are called to do and not go out of focus.

Jesus Christ

The Son of God, God who came down as a man to save the fallen man from the perils of hell

Notable for

The Savior of the Lord, who died for the sins of the world

23

JESUS, THE MESSIAH

THE SON OF GOD SUBMITS HIS SPIRITS TO THE FATHER

Then Jesus shouted, "Father, I entrust my spirit into your hands!" And with those words he breathed his last..
LUKE 23:46 NKJV

The Unexpected Volunteer
There was a prisoner condemned to death for multiple cases of criminal offenses. The final day of execution finally came. Hours begin to pass by, the first hour passed, the second passed, the third and down to 10 minutes to the time of execution. Accepting their own fate and expecting to be executed. 5 more minutes, 4, 3, 2 and 60 seconds more, the executioner's phone rang and the voice on the other end said, "the execution has been canceled and the prisoner has been pardoned and there is a volunteer replacement". His

crucifixion was real, He felt every pain, every blow, and every nail. Jesus as man, was the greatest worshipper of all. His life was all about worship. He came to teach and show how to worship the Lord, and He gave His spirit up in the costliest worship ever - taking upon himself the sins of the world and paying the price with his own blood. This is the summation of the worship at Calvary. Jesus was a volunteer replacement for the sins of others.

A King on the Death Row

There is no pain like knowing the date of death. Those who are on death row face a hard type of pain - the pain of knowing when they would breathe their last. The pain of knowing their death date kills them faster than the pain of execution. Those people, they die many times before their death. There is nothing like the endless nightmares they have before their execution. There is nothing like the mental torture they go through, waking up and breaking up with cold sweat. What Jesus went through was a thorough torture.

As a man, he knew he was going to die. At the garden of Gethsemane - he brought the 3 closest disciples to him and went further down to pray. After prayer, they came to arrest Jesus. He said - *this is the hour that the kingdom of darkness will glory.* In the journey of Jesus, that was that hour that the kingdom of darkness gloried. He said *"my soul is sorrowful"*. The detachment of the spirit from the body is a very painful thing. The pain of Jesus was not the pain of physical stripes, or physical torture at this point, it was the unquantifable agony of the heart. A pain he felt as man and not God yet he went every step of the way in obedience to give up His own body in order to purchase the church, and release sinners into a new freedom by His blood. This truth is often veiled from sinners who are being signed up as believers in Jesus as well as people coming forward to be a part of the lead worship team in church gatherings.

The gospel of Jesus is never bait to entice sinners without laying it bare and let sinners know what they are signing up into when they decide to live the rest of their lives in worship of the Lord Jesus. It is a lifestyle of saying goodbye too worldliness and an entry into a solemn powerful and faithfully obedience Christ-like life, filled with worship.

Gethsemane: The Beginning of Redemption

The road to the cross was very long and lonely. It all began just before Jesus headed to Gethsemane and he predicted His disciples would betray him, to which Peter answered: *"Even if all are made to stumble because of you, I will never be made stumble"* - Mathew 26:33. To which Jesus said to him, " Assuredly I say to you that this night, before the rooster crows, you will deny Me three times".- Matthew 26:34. Peter insisted, *"Even if I had to die with you, I will not deny you!"* - Matthew 26:35. Afterwards he headed to the garden of Gethsemane with His disciples. He went farther out with Peter and two other disciples, telling them to stay and pray along. The disciples could have watched Jesus and pray along; but the cup Jesus was about to drink was not a collective one. Though He asked them to pray with Him, but by the decree of heaven and the justice of God, it was impossible. They were fulfilling the prophecy - "the soul who sins shall die".

Three Nature of God Provided Salvation for Man

The fall of man was anticipated from the foundation of the world. The three natures of God came together and designed the ultimate salvation of man after fall.

1. **Justice:** The nature of God which is justice spoke and said, the wages of sin is death.
2. **Mercy:** The nature of God which is found in His mercy asked; Is there any way that if man falls, justice will still be carried out, yet man will be redeemed?
3. **Wisdom**: The nature of God through the spirit of wisdom say: The only way is for the blood of the Son of God, Jesus Christ, to be shed for the remission of the sins of many.

This was what happened from the battle in Eden was the battle of worship. Man fell and they worshipped the enemy and they lost authority.. The enemy came to sell fake to them. In the garden of Eden, instead of submitting to the sovereignty of God, they followed were self-willed. In the garden of Gethsemane, Jesus said, "Let your will be done." Through self-will Adam lost authority and put the entire world in danger, by the will of God, Jesus saved the world. Another man, by the divine ordination of God said, "the will of the Father. When the different counsels of God came to reason together, justice was there, grace was in there.

Joseph Arimathea: A Helper & Partaker in the Suffering of Christ
There are some worshippers who are called to partake in the suffering of Christ. Very rare to find. Apostle Paul wished to be amongst those, but he was not privileged. He said, that I may know Him and the power of His resurrection, and the fellowship of His sufferings, being conformed to His death - in Philiplians 3:10. People like Joseph Arimathea is a classic example of the worshippers who partake in the sufferings of Jesus. He was a vessel chosen to help Jesus after being afflicted for 3 long days, Joseph Arimathea came to help carry the blood cross.. He did not only give a helping hand to Jesus, he partook in the sacrifice, and in the shame and after fulfilling his assignment, disappeared into the crowd. We see a similar attempt made my Uriah when he tried to support the falling ark; because Uriah was not called, he perished instantly. A call into worship is a mystery too. No man can understand.

`

The Blood
The mystery of life is hidden in the blood. That is the same reason that when the angel of death was passing through Egypt, the children of Israel in the land of Goshen were instructed to kill the lamb. Representing the blood of Jesus that was slain from the foundations of the earth. This signifies the identity of the blood of Jesus sacrificed ahead of them. When the angel of death got to their door post, he saw life and pass over them. Here lies the covenant of

the blood of Jesus revealed through the communion - the bread and wine as the body and the blood of Jesus.

Worship & Sacrifice

Worship is never complete until there is a sacrifice. Worship demands sacrifice and that is why it was needful for the Great High Priest to come down to sacrifice Himself on the altar at Calvary to take away the sins of the entire world. Otherwise, everyone would still have to use the blood of animals to make atonement for their unintentional sins and pay for their preconceived sin with their own blood. Therefore, the requirement of the law that says the soul which sin must die, is fulfilled because of the worship of Jesus - the One who had no sin, dying for us.

A Lifestyle of Worship

Jesus lived the perfect life of worship. He thanked and praised God at every opportunity. The prayers Jesus prayed were not for him alone - Prayer destroys the effect of the sifting of the enemy and prayers restores the believers. Worship, prayers and the word are inseparable; they go together. Jesus lived a perfect life of worship. Every time the Scripture said, "the Son cannot do anything without the father". Saying "I thank you father". He continued a lifestyle of worship.

JESUS' MODEL OF WORSHIP

Jesus came to break the stronghold of religion and legalism. He came to break us free from the prison of templated-worship. He came to break us free from worship that seeks to apply a stipulated set of rules as to how to worship.

As the Lord conversed with the Samaritan woman, comparing or last words of Jesus gives us the format with which Jesus worshipped the Father as He was being sacrificed at Calvary.

A worshipper with a crushed spirit, still loving yet pouring out His blood and hanging on to the price ahead, and yet committing His spirit into Father's hand.

1. **(Mark 15:34)** - *"And at the ninth hour Jesus cried out with a loud voice, 'Eloi, Eloi, lama sabachthani?'* which is translated, 'My God, My God, why have You forsaken Me?'"

2. **(Luke 23:46)** - *"And Jesus, crying out with a loud voice, said, 'Father, into Your hands I commit My spirit.'* And having said this, He breathed His last."

24

THE TABERNACLE: GOD'S SANCTUARY

"Remove the impurities from silver, and the sterling will be ready for the silversmith."

PROVERBS 25:4

Remove iniquity and impurities from the worshipper and the worshipper will be admissible into God's presence. Jesus came to change the way we worship. Rather than going to a physical temple before accessing God's presence, Jesus made way for us to become God's holy temple. The understanding of worship becomes deeper when we study the tabernacle, the earthly tent where God dwelt in the old times. Below is a table with the tabernacle elements and the representation of some of the major articles in the tabernacle and its earthly translation.

The Tabernacle		
Tabernacle Elements	Before	Now

The Bronze Altar	This was were sacrifices were made and the blood of animals were shed for the remission of sins	The first representation of the Bronze Altar was at Calvary where Jesus was sacrificed for the sins of many. The bronzen altar is now the heart of men, from where worship is offered to the Lord in truth and in spirit
The Bronze Laver	The laver was used for cleansing after sacrificed by the priests	Spiritual cleansing and detoxification through fasting
The Golden Lampstand	Provided light inside the dark room aand must be kept on by the priest	The representation of the Holy Spirit
The Table of Show Bread	A consecrate dozen of bread to be ate by the priests (Aaron and his sons)	The Holy Communion
The Altar of Incense	At this altar, the Lord gave a special recipe of incense that must be burned to Him from this altar - Leviticus 30:35-37	Prayers and communication with God
The Ark of the Covenant & The Mercy Seat	Physical representation of God's presence which dwelt in the Holies of holy; from	Today, the Lord abides in the believer and speaks to us directly

	where God speaks to the people	
The Veil	Separated the holy place for the Holies of Holy, separating God from men. The veil set a limit to which men could access God's presence. Only the High Priest could enter beyond the veil, once a year.	The veil of the temple was torn as the Lord Jesus gave up His spirit at Calvary, so that all believers in Jesus now have direct access to the Father without the need of an earthly high priest
The Tabernacle	The tabernacle was a physical and mobile tent, where sacrifices were conducted, over the years, the temple was constructed, still a representation of the first tabernacle. The design of the tabernacle was given by God based on the design of the copy of the original tabernacle in heaven	The Tabernacle is the human body. The human body is now God's dwelling place. In the body, the heart/mind is the most sacred place, a representation of the Holies of holy. The place from where worship flows to God

The Worshipper's Body

The power from the heavenly sanctuary flows into the life of the worshipper. Jesus comes to minister in any sanctuary that surrenders in holiness, with purity of heart, and in truth. Jesus being the minister of the Heavenly sanctuary still comes to minister humbly in our bodily sanctuary. This is why the standards of holiness required of the worshipper must be held up high at all times. False teachers may have lowered the requirements, leading the souls of many into the burning sulphur - but every worshipper, teacher, prophet must continue to evangelize the need to keep the earthly sanctuary holy and free from all defilement. This is where the Great High Priest ministers.

A worshipper must get into a point where they say to God, *"I give you my mouth, I give you my mind, I give you my voice, I give you my entire body"*. When we release all of us to the Lord, the power of the Holy Spirit takes over us without limiting God by our emotions, prejudices, picking one preferred Scripture over the other or translating the instructions of the Lord to us wrongly because of biases - we come to the full adherence of the power of the Holy Ghost and there is no height too High for God to bring us to in worship to reveal His glory to us.

The Worshipper's Giftings

The gift of the Lord is irrevocable. The gift of God is the spirit of God. God is the giver of all gifts. A worshipper must understand this. As a worshipper, the fastest way to lose your connection to God is to exalt your giftings. Many exalt their giftings beyond the Giver of the gift - making a big path for their own fall.

Satan through the spirit of pride is the major enemy of the worshipper. When pride enters a worshipper's heart, the gift given by God is not taken away, but has become perverted. Anything or anyone associated with pride is severely destroyed by the Lord. A worshipper must always be aware that pride is the same thing as stealing God's glory. Pride is stealing the praises meant for God. Our God will never share His glory with anyone and will destroy whoever goes after His glory. One thing to continually ask the Lord is the spirit of humility, a heart that is not fat, but a heart that is bowed down and surrendered to the Lord.

INSIDE THE WORSHIPPER'S HEART

God adorns Himself with holiness. He receives worship that is prepared for Him in holiness. Any worship without holiness is stinking to Him and He abhors it. The heart is the manufacturing center of all ideas that eventually come to life. Every thought is conceived in the heart before it becomes a word or an action. The human heart is situated too be the dwelling place of God.

Building An Altar for Yahweh

If God has called you as a worship minister; a pastor, an evangelist, or to minister in any way in public, you must first have an altar raised up to Yahweh at home. This means there is no public ministry without a private ministry. There is no how you will have the backing of the Lord in public if you have not established a relationship with him privately. The private ministry begins with the person who has kept their physical body - the temple of the living God in the right state before God. Building worship altars sounds simple to the uncircumsized ears, but those who live sacrificially knows that obedience is as costly as the works of building. There is no greater worship than living in righteousness. The worship of rightful living is more acceptable to the Lord than sacrifice.

The Worshipper: A Carrier of The Altar

The worshipper is the sanctuary of God - and inside the sanctuary, there is an altar. The human heart can be called the altar in the altar. The altar of God abodes inside the heart of the worshipper. The heart of the worshipper represents the altar in the sanctuary. The heart being the most sacred part of the human body is the seat of power. The heart is the seat of authority. The heart of a person determines their course of life. This is why God is very concerned about the condition of the human heart.

The heart of man is like a different compartment in a storage place. It could be compared to post office mailboxes that has the ability to hold vital information. Each box has a key and letters will not be mixed up. This is how the heart of a lot of people has been structured . Many people make rules against God in their own hearts saying, Lord you can come to room 101 in my heart, but not to room 102. This brings to remembrance, the Scriptures, when you hear His voice, do not harden your heart. A hardened hard locks up the heart with padlocks and prevents God from reigning in every part of the heart. The Lord is looking for those whose hearts are broken into pieces, those who will not hold back any portion of their heart and who will allow Him move freely in their hearts. Only such hearts do the word of God find highly inflammable.

The Worshipper: Preparing the Altar

A worshipper who carries the Holy altar of the Lord actively prepares the sanctuary and keeps it holy for ministration unto the Lord. God's Holy altar is to be kept sacred at all times, hence, the worshipper understands that it is impossible to complete the arrangement for worship in one hour leading to worship sessions or even 10 hours. Preparation for worship is life long, from the time of our rebirth into the Kingdom of God. Such is the heart of the worshipper; always keeping the altar sacred and ever ready to offer worship.

Part of the worshipper's readiness steps is the intake and consumption of the word of God which is to diligently stored in the heart of the worshipper. When worship is about to begin, the word of God living in the heart beckoned and is used as the primary fire to light the fire on the altar for the fumes and fragrance to be generated. The more word of God in the heart of the worshipper, the bigger the fire gets and the stronger the strength the fire; it gets larger and larger that no one can contain or quench it. The flame gets steady and the sweet aroma goes into distant unknown to reach the throne of God and into the heart of God. And we cannot help but to capture the attention and gain the favor of God. That's what true worship can do. This is the same reason why fire from God's presence descended at the time the priests offered acceptable sacrifice unto the Lord - because the conditions of worship to Yahweh was met. The witness to the presence of God on any living altar is the fire that comes forth after every worship. Just as today; the recipe for the fire is the word of God in the heart of the worshipper. Recall that in Leviticus 10:1 - *Aaron's sons Nadab and Abihu put coals of fire in their incense burners and sprinkled incense over them. In this way, they disobeyed the LORD by burning before him the wrong kind of fire, different than he had commanded.* Any time a strange component is added to worship on Yahweh's altar; there's a mismatch and the Lord would never allow a compromise on His altar.

That is why many sessions termed "worship" today is only a fanfair. Many present day worship teams needs to be disintegrated and recommissioned. Where true worshippers are lacking, pastors can lead their gatherings in God's presence without bringing compromised musicians in. One compromised person on the worship team can bounce the entire congregation of God's presence. Many pastors live in fear that their most talented unrepentant sinner musician would never show up again if they speak the depth of the word of God to them and have them take a break from the worship team, hence polluting the altar. All God asks for is the sacredness of the altar, and of the priests ministering to Him upon those altars. Even where there are no musicians, when the congregants clap their hands or beat their tambourines to worship - will the sound of their claps and tambourine and the right conditions of their hearts not please the Lord?

The Worshipper on The Altar

The worshipper's heart is an altar. When a worshipper worships at a physical altar. For example: when a worshipper worships at a church altar, or at a family altar. There are two altars present at once. The mystery to this is that both altars have to be in its purest form before the Lord. If a worshipper stands on a physical altar with an unclean heart, there is a pollution. There is also a tendency for pollution when a clean heart (the inner altar) is brought upon a filthy altar.

Inner altars

Inner altar is the altar of the human heart. The state of the human heart or mind is a compass that can help tell the direction and quality of worship offered from within that altar. The state of the human mind does not look anything close to facial expressions. The status of the heart is so important to God that He spoke to many of His prophets about the hearts of the people He sent them to. The status of our inner altars is paramount that the Prophet Elijah was sent to reconcile the hearts of the lost children back to the Father. Worship can only break through and saturate the contrite heart through the cracks in the broken heart. The heart becomes thoroughly soaked in the rivers of His presence. This is the critical point where hearts are reconciled back to God. The status of the heart is very vital because there is much that is released into the heart of the worshipper to be birthed on earth - and the name of the Lord will not be defiled or blasphemed. the worshipper, music of heaven is being released unto the earth. The anointed worshipper will always be the channel through which new songs are birthed through.

Types of Inner Altars

There was a sister who the Lord commissioned into worship in 2016. She was anointed and the Holy Spirit would move when she led worship. After we had moved into the assignment at LightHill. She attended one of our Prophetic Worship encounters. The Lord gave me a word for her, and it went thus; *"Sister, stop allowing dead flies to perch on your destiny. You carry a glorious destiny and that has a tendency to attract a lot of flies. If you will give your life to me, I will use you in ways unexpected"*.

We called her to guide her and get her to wait on God and focus on Him while she waits for God's planned marriage. Months later we reached out to her prior to our quarterly 6-hours Worship in 2017; we invited her to come and be a part of the worship team to minister to the Lord. After inviting her, the Lord said; "do you know what she's been doing with her life or do you know her current spiritual state"? My wife, Abigail reached out to her to cancel the invite, then she said she meant to call to say she could not attend the event. Barely two months after *6-hour Worship*, we heard the news she had eloped with one of the married pastors in the church she attended.

Stories of promiscuity, strife, control and pride is very common across worship teams. The root causes of all these are hardly dealt with. There are forces contending against worship. The moment a worshipper decides in their heart to worship the Lord. They give an additional reason for the enemy to attack them. The spiritually unminded worshipper will be dragged into a ditch that is impossible to get out from. The decision to worship God is never to be taken lightly because the enemy will attempt to deter through different avenues.

The condition of the heart in worship is a major determination of how far a worshipper can get in worship. There are various types of hearts and some are listed below:

Prideful Heart: Worship and pride never goes together. The spirit of pride pushes people to run away from discipline. Pride hardly shows up to the person it is at work. Pride is designed to be stealth. How can a person uncover the spirit of pride? For someone who God answers their prayers. They will only see God as the prayer answering person who is financially stable will see God as the financial provided. For someone who has lived all their lives in righteousness, they will see the holiness of God. The main opposition that a prideful heart faces is God Himself. Pride is an abomination in the kingdom of God. No proud heart has a chance with God. Pride and the worship of the Living God have nothing in common. A worshipper is placed in an elevated and honorable position in the heart of God. A prideful heart is wrapped in disgrace, shame and destruction - all sponsored by the Lord. The fastest way the devil can destroy a worshipper is to sneak pride into their heart. The fall of the proud does not happen on the day of their fall, the fall took place on the day they opened their heart to pride.

The subject of pride is very important for the worshipper to understand. Aa prideful heart seeks to exalt itself. A prideful heart elevates itself. A prideful heart seeks to accept worship and steal the glory that belongs to God alone. That is why there is an automatic punishment for every prideful heart, and that punishment is destruction.

Veiled Hearts - Hearts that cannot see the goodness in the works of the hand of the Lord. *Lamentations 3:65 Give them a veiled heart; our curse be upon them!* A veiled heart has no revelation of God. There is no revelation of the gospel of Jesus. It is said concerning the veiled hearts, " *the ears is ever hearing but never understanding*". A veiled heart cannot worship the Lord because it has no revelation of the Lord to be worshipped.

Enslaved Heart: An enslaved heart is the heart that is held bound in chains. Hearts that are enslaved are held down in captivity - as a slave to something else. An enslaved heart cannot enter into the worship of Yahweh. An enslaved heart is a heart where fornication, adultery, wine dwells -- *Hosea 4:11 Hearts of fornication, adultery, "Harlotry, wine, and new wine enslave the heart.*

Perverted Heart: A perverted heart leans towards everything that is not acceptable by God. A perverted heart works against the laws of God having fashioned wrongs as right and right asa politically incorrect. Perversion is what makes people see no good in righteousness and adopt evil instead. Perversion is what makes people falsely accuse the innocent, a perverted heart is always on the wrong and opposing side of the word of God. The perverted heart will not come anywhere near God in worship, for God hates. The Scripture describes the way of the perverted heart and God's hatred for a heart that is perverted in the passage below.

Proverbs 6:12-19

What are worthless and wicked people like? They are constant liars, signaling their deceit with a wink of the eye, a nudge of the foot, or the wiggle of fingers. Their perverted hearts plot evil, and they constantly stir up trouble. But they will be destroyed suddenly, broken in an instant beyond all hope of healing. There are six things the Lord hates—no, seven things he detests: haughty eyes, a lying tongue, hands that kill the innocent, a heart that plots evil, feet that race to do wrong, a false witness who pours out lies, a person who sows discord in a family.

Any heart in the perversion state will not get through to the Lord in worship. Worship arising from the pervert in heart is offered to the devil.

Stony Heart: A stony heart is a callous heart. A heart that shows no compassion or mercy, a stony heart is a hardened heart. A stony heart is an uncaring heart, a heart without feelings of empathy for others. Hardened hearts are stony hearts. Stony hearts cannot see the Lord in worship. Despite all the works of the Lord revealed through the hands of Moses, Pharaoh refused to know the Lord or allow God's people to worship the Lord. A hardened heart has been desensitized that it is totally dead in sin. Despite all the works of the Lord revealed through the hands of Moses, Pharaoh refused to know the Lord or allow God's people to worship the Lord. This was a classic example of a stony heart. A hardened heart cannot get into the presence of the Lord in worship. A stony heart must be broken for worship to flow through.

Filthy Heart: When a heart is in the state of filthiness, the heart is in a dirty state oozing out stench that are displeasing to the Lord. A filthy heart is contaminated and in a state of decay. A filthy heart is like a storage of dung. A heart filled with lustful desires, sexual immorality, unholy passions, drunkenness, orgies is not a habitable or desirable place for the Lord in worship. One of the easiest way for a heart to get into filitiness is pornography. Except a heart is cleansed fromfiltiness, there is no worship going to the Lord.

Disloyal Heart: A disloyal heart has turned slightly or completely away from the Lord. They are influenced by other gods or will support the worship of other Gods like SOlomon did and was recorded in I Kings 11:4 - *For it was so, when Solomon was old, that his wives turned his heart after other gods; and his heart was not loyal to the Lord his God, as was the heart of his father David.* Many believers still shout out to their unbelieving friends during their religious festivals and allowing their hearts to depart from complete faithfulness to the Living God.

There are many blatant idolaters with bold declarations of idol worship. Some worship the sun, the moon, the stars, and everything else but the Living God. They are not worshippers of Yahweh and do not pretend to be. However, many of those who have declared their faithfulness to Jesus still go to watch masquerade display, partake in sallah meat sacrificed at salah times, or go for palm reading, dabble into astrology. God detests adultery. He wants those that are called by His name who will worship Him have a distinguishable boundary, know and identify the God they serve; so they are not sitting down in between. Elijah said in 1 Kings 18:21; *Elijah went before the people and said, "How long will you waver between two opinions? If the LORD is God, follow him; but if Baal is God, follow him." But the people said nothing.*

The state of the heart is of great significance to God in worship that the Scripture heavily references the statuses of the hearts and more is referenced in Ephesians 4:17-24.

This I say, therefore, and testify in the Lord, that you should no longer walk as the rest of the Gentiles walk, in the futility of their mind, having their understanding darkened, being alienated from the life of God because of the ignorance that is in them, because of the blindness of their heart; who, being past feeling, have given themselves over to lewdness, to work all uncleanness with greediness. But you have not so learned Christ, if indeed you have heard Him and have been taught by Him, as the truth is in Jesus: that you put off, concerning your former conduct, the old man which grows corrupt according to the deceitful lusts, and be renewed in the spirit of your mind, and that you put on the new man which was created according to God, in true righteousness and holiness.

The double-heart, the deceitful heart, the crafty heart, the darkened heart, the stony heart, the corrupt heart, the lustful heart, the futile heart - all of these kinds of hearts cannot host God's presence in worship. Until a person becomes selfless and say to God in prayers:

1. Lord, would you break my heart for what breaks yours?
2. Would you rend my heart for what rend yours?
3. Let your will be done first in me
4. Let your kingdom come, first in me
5. Build me up as your sanctuary

These are the prayers of the worshipper seeking to feel the emotions of God. With this prayer, we ask the Lord, "Father, let me feel your emotions". Worship gives us access into the heart of the Father. Asking to feel the emotions of God is asking for your heart to be united with the heart of the Lord such that you feel what the Father feels, and the Lord's mind is revealed to you. The Father's heart is tender, loving, faithful and merciful. This is why it is impossible for anyone whose heart looks nothing like God's to breakthrough in worship. When a heart is beautiful and scents nicely to God, this is when the Lord can make such heart His holy altar and His dwelling place.

A New Heart

A new heart is required for anyone intending to give worship to the Lord. The old heart needs to be put out and a new heart is required. The old heart is no longer of use because the content of the old heart had corrupted the entire heart. A new heart is therefore required. A new heart looks nothing like the old.

Ezekiel 36:24-17

For I will take you from among the nations, gather you out of all countries, and bring you into your own land. Then I will sprinkle clean water on you, and you shall be clean; I will cleanse you from all your filthiness and from all your idols. I will give you a new heart and put a new spirit within you; I will take the heart of stone out of your flesh and give you a heart of flesh. I will put My Spirit within you and cause you to walk in My statutes, and you will keep My judgments and do them.

The Lord is always willing to give new hearts out. He is always willing to take away every heart that looks nothing like the one he desires. A worshipper cannot harbor hate, bitterness, jealousy, strife, malice and every works of the flesh. For the sake of the worshipper, He went to the cross of Calvary to nail every work of flesh to the cross.

The Desirable Hearts in Worship

Before spiritual and truthful worship begins, a clean heart is created in the worshipper. A heart that trembles and fears the Lord. A heart cleaned with the washing of the water and the blood of Jesus. The heart is renewed, totally transformed and is upright before the Lord at all times. A heart that is wholly consecrated to the Lord. A heart that boldy says to the Lord, "I will worship you with my whole heart". A heart that will never box out the Lord from any part of it. A heart that will open up all the compartments of the heart and let God all have it. A heart that will not limit God by restricting God into certain areas. AA heart that will not say to the Lord, you can only dwell in a certain square foot of my heart, but a heart that is fully in submission to the Lord.

The Lord wants a tender, broken and contrite heart in worship. Worship grabs the attention of God. It gives hope. When a man or woman with a contrite heart worships God in the midst of brokenness of heart. Here is why many worshippers who have met the Lord break down in tears in worship. Such tears wipe clean the soul.Tears are like the reset button for the soul. When it's shed in worship, it takes away clutter from the path of worship. Worship needs to be cultivated in the heart. It's like you have a portion of land whose fallow land needs to be tilled to bear much fruit. It involves overturning the surface and getting the heart ready for planting seeds - the seed being the word of God; and the seed needs watering and grooming to generate worship as fruits. A heart that has no barriers for Him, one where His spirit could flow all through. A circumcised heart is one that has undergone the surgery of the Lord. One that harbors no contention, strife, anger, lust or evil. he wants a circumscribed heart - such hearts the Father desires in worship and never holds back from such hearts.

SECTION THREE

JOURNEYING INTO THE DEPTHS OF WORSHIP

25

WORSHIP &
THE CHURCH

GOD'S PURPOSE FOR HIS LIVING CHURCH ON EARTH

God's purpose in all this was to use the church to display his wisdom in its rich variety to all the unseen rulers and authorities in the heavenly places. This was his eternal plan, which he carried out through Christ Jesus our Lord.

EPHESIANS 3:10-11 NLT

Jesus has paid the price with His blood and He has become the head of the church, and the church becoming His body. The purpose of the church is that the church will be able to work in the divine wisdom of God, and the plans of God will be fulfilled through the empowerment of the church on earth.

The church, one is in God's intentional worship is the only organization on earth that has been given the power of the manifold wisdom of God such that the whole world goes to learn of the mysteries of heaven and of God through the church. Here is why the entry of the church into a territory is one that comes in power. When the church successfully enters a city, a province or a nation; there must be a positive influence   measurable by economic growth, standard of living, lower rates of immorality, improved facilities and more. The church has been given powers to build nations, reveal heaven's innovation on earth, crown kings and build kingdoms, set free from slavery and bring God's kingdom on earth. The church's purpose is to cultivate worshippers.   This is part of the Church's purpose on earth.

The church that has gone out of purpose is like a bride of gold, dressed in all her glory, waiting for the bride. While in wait, the bride drags her glory on the floor and takes off her glorious robe, and goes naked. This is the situation of any church that has steered off it primary calling.

Swapping God's Truth for Lies

Every worshipper of Yahweh must be aware that witchcraft is all out against their mission to worship Yahweh. Nothing destroys the ministry of a worshipper faster than ignorance of witchcraft and attempting to deal with the spirit of witchcraft in a gentle manner. If you want to enter and stay in worship, you need to defeat witchcraft.

Witchcraft thrives in secrecy; and fights against the building up and maintaining true worship because with worship comes revelation. Worship takes the worshipper into the mind of the Father; and every concealed information is revealed, the hidden glory of the Lord that is concealed is revealed to the worshipper.

Witchcraft has mastered over hundreds and thousands of years how to detract people out of worship. Witchcraft will never blatantly declare a war against worship, but uses cunningness to lure people into something else resembling worship but is not the worship of Yahweh. Unfortunately, there are a lot of those gatherings put together to deceive people out of the true worship of Yahweh. Many worshippers have become a casualty of war because they did not search deeper in the Lord what worship really means.

Beyond the foundational covenants

When you breakthrough the foundational covenants that prevents people from entering into worship, you enter into your worship ministry. However, once you're entering into worship, there is another entity waiting to chase you out of God's presence in worship, that is the satanic institution of witchcraft. This is why many people genuinely enter into worship and the fire in them is quenched and their ministry is short-lived.

The minister who heard the call of God into the ministry of worship. They began to worship the Lord and new songs from heaven was released consistently to them. Suddenly miracles of all sorts began to happen and more worship ministers began to join the team. Suddenly there was a sister who was a worshipper as well with 20 years experience on the worship team. The moment she came into the worship team, the worship team seem to be thriving; worship events hosted by the team were successful because of her expertise in organization and management. She brought in experiences from other worship ministries. When the worship leader received inspiration that seem weird, the sister would say, "this is how they did it at my former church" and they would go with the sister's suggestion. Not quite long, revelation disappeared. Though the worship minister was not involved in unholy relations with anyone, he wondered why God moving in their midst like He did originally - the reason can be found in Exodus 25:40 *"Be sure that you make everything according to the pattern I have shown you here on the mountain.* God has a plan for every ministry, and He will reveal His plans to the worship leader He has set in place to lead the mission. In the plan will also contain the pattern that must be followed in ministry, therefore there is a unique pattern for every call. If the original pattern is neglected and some other person's plan or suggestion is picked up, God is no longer obligated to fulfill that plan, and most times He departs from the mission.

Satan understands that obedience is better than sacrifice. When the Lord has called a ministry and given a ministry the assignment of "restoring holiness into a city". The Lord may begin to show the leader of the mission ways to help people learn about holiness.

The Church & Worship

Where you see the worship team tearing apart, where you see war in the choir, where you see adultery, fornication flying around on the worship team, the foundation has not been dealt with. No amount of conversation settlements will resolve these kinds of problems. The devil will do everything, including tearing apart a Church to prevent through worship. The only way to go is a foundational warfare. If you pastor a church and you have not addressed the idolatry issues in your foundation, your enter congregation will not enter into the worship of God. You may think you're in worship already, but you will be able to tell by results.

The first day I told our former pastor, I said to him, "there are raw talents in the choir, but there is a lot of work to do". He said, "there is massive work to do". "He said we have a worship leader, but he is trying hard to put it all together but we will be glad if you can help him out". I teamed up with worship leader. The first worship meeting we had, the members of the team were fighting over who gets the microphone; and the worship leader looked on helplessly. I called the worship leader to put his team in place but they would not listen to him. In the 3rd week, order was slowly returning. We were to dress uniformly, fast the days preceding ministrations, be punctual at meetings and get into deep prayers before each ministration. People who were timid because they thought they needed a specific pitch of voice to sing began to come forth to lead worship, having realized that singing is not necessarily worship. The entire church noticed and they would come after service to say to us; the worship has changed, we feel the power of God. Certain people dropped off the worship team because they did not want to dress in uniform. There were bold witchcraft manifestations in the church set to prevent worship. The hand of God moved during worship and there was the sound of revival. By the second month, the Lord began to speak expressly to the church leaders about witchcraft; by the third month, the church had splitted. The unaddressed spirit of witchcraft in a church will go to any length to falsify worship or prevent true worship altars from being built.

Idols and The Worship Team

For the power of the Lord to come to abide in a worship gathering, you need to dethrone demonic ancient gods. A lot of people never return a second time when they are told that they need to undergo deliverance and fast before they join our worship team. The people may have no clue, but the spirits in them hate getting caught and they never want to depart. So they push their victims around, and feel very comfortable wherever they cannot be found out so as to continue doing the works of pollution.Â

The hard truth is that if thereâ€™s one who is still tied to the gods in their foundation on a worship team, thereâ€™s likely to be pollution. The idol in them will never submit to theÂ Holy Spirit. When the Holy Spirit is calling the team to worship in a certain way, the demonic deity will speak up and say things like: *we do not worship God for more than 20 minutes in our former church, why are we spending 1 hour in worship?*Â They will always be used against the worship of Yahweh. They will be igniters of strife, if not that; pride will overcome them, if not pride, other vices will lure them out of Godâ€™s presence.

How Witchcraft Destroys Worship

Witchcraft comes to lure worshippers out of their calling. Witchcraft comes to say, "I've been in ministry for 20 years, here's the way we do it". Any unsuspecting worshipper who lays down God's pattern shown to them and adopts the plan presented by the spirit of witchcraft is thrown out of Yahweh's presence immediately and witchcraft takes over from that day forward. The worshipper who does not bow to the spirit of witchcraft is sorely detested by witchcraft agents. In raging, they rage violently; in a church settings, they leave church because their plans to taint and pollute worship was destroyed. Some of them are positioned as "evangelists" who help spread the works of God under a mission. If plans to soil worship fail, they do reversal evangelism, undoing evangelism they once did and misleading others. Many pastors are being held captive; and they take every suggestion in for the fear of losing a strategic influencer in the church. Wrong! In building worship altars for Yahweh, you cannot an altar to delight or please people. Remember you're building for Yahweh, many who do not walk in spirit may not be pleased at the level of holiness required. Some will suggest that you sing songs and dance the dances in ways that Yahweh has not called you to. The moment you submit to those suggestions, that would be the end of the worship anointing as the presence of God does not tarry in disobedience.

Many worship ministers know that they were called into worship. They even remember their encounters with the Lord, however, they found that they no longer hear from God. The truth is that the spirit of God never informs a person that they have departed.

How Witchcraft Destroys Worship

There is no worship mission that is not confronted by witchcraft powers. Unfortunately, many missionaries are waiting for a strange person to walk in to their mission as witches and wizards when the witch activated to destroy worship is their father, mother, brother, sister, son, daughter, who carry the same DNA as them. Many worship ministers are looking and searching for where the witchcraft attacking their ministry is when the witchcraft is working in full force in the wife or husband.

God led an individual to our ministry. This individual was a minister. Things were turned upside down in their life. When we began to pray concerning this individual, God said to us concerning him, *"what is the use of a person who is supposed to be the salt of the earth, but their salt has become worthless that it is not even fit for the dunghill?* The

Lord said further, "*this is what happens to a person who lays down the anointing of God over their lives and go to seek after worldliness. They get what they pay for.* This person's life had gone totally into a mess, one that was beyond description. Their spouse operated in deep witchcraft and their life was in great danger. This was supposed to be God's worshipper, a priest of God. However, the spouse they ended up with was assigned solely to them to make sure they never get close to God's presence in worship. Any moment the individual decides to worship, pray or fast, the spouse has other programs arranged to prevent worship. Any time this individual looks for a way to take time to fast, pray and worship, the spouse rages violently complaining of the spiritual state of the individual, and the individual fearfully stays away from seeking God so they can please their spouse.

There are a few versions of these tactics that God has brought to our notice. There is another situation where the woman of the household pretends to be deeply involved in the things of God, however, she was not. Anytime the husband was about to fast, or spend more time with God, she will throw tantrums and bring up fights. These fights will eventually lure the husband out of worship.

Another one was the situation where a parent who is a church elder was hiding under the cover of a "church elder" but they were deeply involved in witchcraft, afflicting their spouse and children. The child is a minister and God began to say to us, if they do not break the witchcraft stronghold and influence from their parents, they would not survive in ministry. There is no continuity in ministry until witchcraft is fought and destroyed.

This is why every man or woman who has a ministry assignment is a greater target for bewitchment. Many agents of witchcraft are sent out to marry anointed worshippers, to detract them from worship. A minister whom we ministered to was in deep problems. He stopped by occasionally to join us in prayers. Then recently, he joined us again for one of our weekly services. After the service, we began to pray; the Lord said concerning him, *"this is what happens to an anointed man who abandons the oil upon his head and places a woman above God, they end up marrying a witch"*. We asked the minister of God, and he said that was true. He said his wife was not comfortable at his former church;hence they left. It seemed to have become a pattern; the wife was luring him out of every gathering where the power of the Holy Spirit was present. The Lord said to him during the ministration, *"do not think your wife does not know what is happening right now as you're seeking the counsel of the Lord"*. The minister of God was seeking deliverance for his family. He said the wife says he's too spiritual; and tends towards worldliness, alcoholism, adultery and emotional blackmail As we finished ministration, to our surprise, his wife was on the phone and wanted to speak to us. On the phone; she said, *"what is the prayer my husband praying for? His prayers is too much. He is overly praying, and his prayers is taking out of their family time. Where does the word of God ask him to pray, why does our family need prayer?, The prayer is too much"*. This is what witchcraft does. However, the witchcraft spirit in the wife was very blatant.

Witchcraft & Bias

Unfortunately many worshippers remain in the state of belief and continue to wonder whether it is true that the witchcraft attack against them is from a close family relation or a close person in their network. Before they get out of their state of unbelief, witchcraft may have already destroyed many in their bias. Witchcraft do not immediately destroy, but bias does. King Asa of Israel didn't allow bias to ruin his mission to restore worship altars. He had to displace his own grandmother for the mission to succeed. *"Also he removed Maachah his grandmother from being queen mother, because she had made an obscene image of Asherah. And Asa cut down her obscene image and burned it by the Brook Kidron. But the high places were not removed.*

Nevertheless Asa's heart was loyal to the LORD all his days. He also brought into the house of the LORD the things which his father had dedicated, and the things which he himself had dedicated: silver and gold and utensils." I Kings 15:13-15 NKJV

26

WORSHIP &
THE WORD

THE WORSHIPPER PRAISES THE WORD OF GOD

> In God, *whose* word I praise,
> In the Lord, *whose* word I praise,

PSALM 56:10

Worship is the only currency in the presence of the Lord. Without being founded and grounded in the Word, the worshipper is misguided. The worshipper must be constantly washed by the word and watered by the word, otherwise they run dry. When a worshipper is planted deep in the Word, then worship comes from the throne of grace , energized by the Holy Spirit, through the heart of men back into the throne of God. When people read the word of God, it's kept in their lives. When people read the word of God and then go to worship the Lord. Fire comes down from the throne of God, and that fire ignites the word from within the life of the person. It is the fire that kindles the incense. The incense does not just come by itself. It is the fire that comes - the worship that mixes with the word starts a fire. Whoever worships without the word of God is emptiness. If the word

221

of God is not evident, it is emptiness, and it hurts them, because the fire that starts has nothing to consume. It eats deep. That's why you have frustrated worshippers with good voice, tear-evoking worshippers, yet, no power comes from them. Everything is hinged upon the foundation of the word of God. When the word of God is so evident in the life of any man or woman, when worship comes in, it ignites. When the altar of worship is raised with the understanding and the background of the word, it sparks fire. The fire is the fire that burns the incense. Once the incense is in, worship with the word becomes prayer. That is when the Holy Ghost begins to pray for God's people with groaning that cannot be understood. It is a process. You must understand. Worship without the word is emptiness says the Lord. The enemy shoots arrow at the mind of people so that the mind is not calm and collective to worship God.

Daniel informs us, "I, Daniel understand by books". The revelation of the knowledge of God comes from the word of God. How best to know God than to read directly from His inspired writings? How can one worship a God we have never seenm?. Without the word of God in us, there is no fire to kindle the sacrifice of worship. At the moment a sinner encounters the Lord, it's the word of God heard that shines as light and gives their heart the revelation of God, causing a crushing down of a heart that was once stony.

The word of God is as a lamp. Every worshipper must rely on the word for revelation. Without the word of God, worship does not go beyond the surface. The word of God is compared to an implantation able to save and help get rid of all types of moral filth in James 1:2. You can attain sustenance in worship through the word of God. Hebrews 1:3 indicates that the word of God is an insulation for sustenance.

The Realm of the Word

There are major realms of the Word of God that a worshipper can enter into. With the ingestion of the words of God and the power of the Holy Spirit, revelation is granted to the worshipper. To an ordinary ear, the songs of angels may seem boring after learning that the highest levels of angels, around the throne of God cover their faces, and their legs and say "Holy Holy, Holy" at all times. The mind of the non-worshipper may find it weird, but the worshipper with the revelation through the Word of God understands that when a bit of the vastness of God is revealed, speech may not be needed and silence, and that silence, may be imputed as worship too.

#1 **The Water of the Word** – Isaiah 55:10 compares the word of God to the rain water. When a person is at this level, it is similar to the time of salvation when the water of the word spoken to them brings life into the deadness in their lives. At the water level, dead things are brought back to life.

#2 **The Milk of the Word** – As milk is for believers, so is the realm of the milk of the Word 1 Peter 2: 2 . After the water of the word has worked and has brought life into the new believer, the new believer is fed with the milk of the word of God. The milk of the word helps the new worshipper know is right and not in the Kingdom. At the milk stage, they learn the elements of their faith. Here is why many believers never gets beyond the salvation encounter, because they dwell at this level, feeding on infant milk, and unable to ingest solid food yet. they will never be able to go into the level of uprooting strongholds and rebuilding the ancients altars of worship. Apostle Paul could speak in depth at Corinth, he only spoke to them as babes because they still fed on milk. Apostle Paul knew their capacity and what they cannot receive.

#3 **The Realm Meat of the Word -** This is the realm of the solid food. *But solid food is for the mature, who by constant use have trained themselves to distinguish good from evil* - Hebrews 5:14. This is where the worshipper has been trained and tested knows whaaat is right from wrong.

#4 The Realm of the Honey of the Word : Highlighted in Psalm 119:103 and Proverbs 24:13. The Word of God was compared to honey. A worshipper gets to a place where the word of God becomes like honey to their soul. This is where you've been asking God for wisdom, and He shows you a scripture about wisdom and folly, and you discovered you have exhibited actions that qualifies as foolish according to the word of God, and you take it joyfully and submit yourself to work on you.

#5 The Realm of the Wine of the Word: Wine is an intoxicant. It is a product design to alter the state of the mind. One who is intoxicated is not only a danger to themselves but to others. The first appearance of the Holy Ghost in the books of Acts 2 was a depiction of intoxication. They were intoxicated with the wine of the Holy spirit. When you get to a certain realm, when you feast with the word, you can no longer control yourself, you live by the word. That is why there is no how a wine can be strong that the intoxicated will last for a week. You have to come back for daily intoxication. This is with the word of God, you need to go back for refilling.

#6 The Realm of the Fire of the Word: This realm is the highest realm in the word of God. Jeremiah said in his lamentation, *But if I say, "I will not mention his word or speak anymore in his name," his word is in my heart like a fire, a fire shut up in my bones. I am weary of holding it in; indeed, I cannot.* - Jeremiah 20:9. *The word of God gets so hot and becomes fire in the life of the worshipper.* The worshipper is who is a prophet will get the message out to the people just as the Lord wants it delivered. They will not look at the faces of the people or think of diluting the message, but the word goes out as fire. The Bible teacher who is in this realm will begin to fire out arrows when they teach the word of God, and the enemies of God will be dispersed. The musician who is at this level will begin to blow, or play the word of God in their instruments, and they fill the air in the atmosphere with the word of

God and darkness vanishes. The school teacher who is at this level goes to school to teach her students, and her lessons transforms her students lives. The employee who at this stage goes to a new place of work and the employer begins to prosper. The carrier of the word of God is highly charged with power. Agents of darkness hate such worshippers, because of the powerful fire all around them.

Any worshipper can move successfully through the stage, it all begins with a seed, and the seed is the word of God. The word of God is like a seed. The power of the Holy Spirit acts upon the seed and waters it. As the seed grows, worshippers enter into different realms. This is where understanding comes to place. That is why there is a power that comes upon your tongue when demons to attack that you you decree death upon it. Look at the Peter, after feasting on the word of God, He received boldness and spoke in confidence and 3000 people were added to the church.

Meditation & Worship

A lot of the troubles people go through is inability to internalize the word. It is important to internalize the word of God. The word of God is internalized through meditation. Without meditation, the believer is unable to get into worship. What do we meditate on? We meditate on the word of God. The word of God reveals who God is, His ways, His laws, what He has done, what He will do what He delights in, what He abhors and His plans for us.

What is meditation?

Meditation is the passage through which the spirit of God in God's word flows from our soul to our spirit for the purpose of spiritual growth. Meditation is a process of implanting of the word of God into your spirit. Meditation is spiritually feeding on the word of God. The human mind constantly engages in meditation whether we know it or not. You may meditate on your day, on your relationship with your friend or loved ones. One of the things that make a significant difference in the lives of innovators is the ability to

225

meditate on subjects of interest. When we meditate on the word of God, our minds receive a deeper opening into realms of wisdom. Without meditation on the word of God, there is no knowledge of the glory of the Lord.

Through meditation on the word of God, the word of God becomes the basis of your thought. In meditation, the word of God is cultivated in you. As a seed, when the word grows, it becomes like a fruitful tree played by the rivers and that is why the Scripture says out of your belly shall flow rivers of living water.

Spiritual Malnourishment

Spiritual Malnourishment is a state where we are not getting the right nutrients to grow spiritually or living life according to God's plan. A spiritually malnourished person is a candidate for spiritual infirmities and attacks. - (Psalm 107:20 He sent out his word and healed them; he rescued them from the grave).

Spiritual malnourishment occurs when there is the lack of consumption of spiritual food which is the word of God. 1 Peter 2:2 says - Like newborn babies, crave pure spiritual milk, so that by it you may grow up in your salvation. Without the right nutrition, a baby cannot grow. A new born baby would be starved and get sick or even die without the right without the right and balanced nutrition.

It is the same for a newborn believer in Christ. The same for a person who backslides. The spirit of God in such people become hungry and thirsty; if the spirit is not revived on time through the word of God, spiritual death occurs.

A spiritually malnourished person cannot worship the Lord in truth and in spirit. The Lord told the Israelites in the book of Leviticus - " fire from other sources are not allowed to be used in worship". The children of Aaron were consumed when they used the foreign recipe for strange fire and offered worship unto YHWH. The recipe used in worship at the time will be equivalent to the word of God in these times. The Lord said to Jeremiah, "Does not the word of God burn as fire"? If therefore the word of God is fire, then the only fire that is permitted to ignite worship is the fire of the word of God. If you don't have the word of God in your heart, then your heart is occupied with something else. It cannot be empty. Either worries, anxieties and cares of this world, jealousy, envy, hate --- you can never never worship with a heart that carries a strange fire.

Determining spiritual malnourishment

An individual might be spiritually malnourished if ...

- They are not getting nutrients from the word of God when they read the Bible but have no revelation from the Holy Spirit after reading.
- Easily distracted when studying the word of God.
- No revelation from the word of God
- Falling into sin from time to time
- Forgetting what has been read from Bible study
- Unable to apply the word of God into daily living

27

WORSHIP & PRAYERS

WORSHIPPING THROUGH PRAYERS

"Then another angel, having a golden censer, came and stood at the altar. He was given much incense, that he should offer it with the prayers of all the saints upon the golden altar which was before the throne. And the smoke of the incense, with the prayers of the saints, ascended before God from the angel's hand".

REVELATION 8:3-4 NKJV

One of the testimonies we love to share is one of a sister who was a part of our worship gathering back in 2017. Doctors found blood in her colon which indicated that there might be a bigger problem at play. They schedule her for a procedure after discovering blood in her colon more than once. A day before the procedure, she called for prayers. As we were about to begin prayers, I heard God say, *"Don't pray, worship me"*. We worshipped through songs for about 15 minutes on the phone and the next day she went in for her procedure. During her pre-operation check, the doctors found no blood. She had been healed.

Prayer and Worship: The Connection

Worship began on earth before prayers began. Abel offered sacrifice before the mention of prayers. Prayers came after wickedness multiplied. Prayers dwells inside of worship. Worship places the mind of the worshipper into a perpetual posture of prayers. With praise on the lips of the worshipper and the word of God in their hearts, the worshipper's prayer is ordered by the mind of God. Prayers coming from worship are not premeditated, they are not sinful or selfish prayers, they coming out of worship are called "Prophetic Prayer". They are prophetic in nature, prayers birthed by the Holy Spirit from inside the core of the heart of the Father. People might wonder, where do our prayers go? The prayers of God's people is offered as worship to the Lord as described in Revelation 8:3-4. Prayer is indeed worship. When prayer is not understood as worship, it becomes transactional and people often relate to God from a place of selfishness. In worship, a worshipper is shown the heart of the Father and is empowered to pray the will of the Father by the Holy Spirit. Many people pray off the will of God asking for ungodly desires and offering abominable prayers. However, in worship, the Father through the Holy Spirit tells the worshipper, here's what's in my heart and here's what you need to ask me - and the worship sends that requests across, a requests that is of the Father. This is sometimes why some prayers are not as effective as others. A person who lives their life as worship unto God will pray differently than a person who only seeks to use God and kiss God goodbye after their needs are met.

Worship: A Mighty Weapon of War

Deliverance ministers have been given access to understand that one of the most potent weapons of warfare is worship and praise. Worship is a weapon that can be taken into any enemy territory to dispossess the enemy. The Holy Spirit leads many deliverance sessions to go into warfare through worship for strong reasons. This is one of the endless benefits released to a worshipper. The worshipper is loaded with atomic weapons in worship. This is the same reason Judah leads Israel into warzones and conquer. In prayer sessions, when the worshipper begins prayers with praise, the war is already declared victory in heaven. The mystery to this revelation is this: In worship, the worshipper is only a vessel, the Holy Spirit is only leading the worshipper who is a vessel of worship in certain actions like words to exalt the Lord with, dances or songs to sing or actions to take - but the main minister in the worshipper's body is the Lord Jesus - who is worshipping the Father in the worshipper's sanctuary. The fight is no longer the worshipper's, but of the Lord. This leads us to the question: what enemy dare bring war into God's Holy place? This is why the devil and its host of demons can not take the heat when the worship of God is quite intense, they flee.

28

WORSHIP, MUSIC, & SOUNDS

WORSHIPPING THROUGH PRAYERS

> *"Then another angel, having a golden censer, came and stood at the altar. He was given much incense, that he should offer it with the prayers of all the saints upon the golden altar which was before the throne. And the smoke of the incense, with the prayers of the saints, ascended before God from the angel's hand".*

REVELATION 8:3-4 NKJV

There are many activities that can lead into worship, however there is a special place for music in worship. Music is able to cut across the spirit, body and soul of a worshipper at the same time and bring be taken into God's presence faster. Worship through pure and consecrated music can usher in God's presence. Worship through songs is defined as songs sang into the heart of the holy spirit from the heart of the Father to the worshipper, back to the Father. Worship through musical sounds is defined as sounds blown into the heart of the Holy Spirit from the heart of the Father to the worshipper, back to the Father. Worship through words and lyrics is defined as words spoken into the heart of the Holy Spirit from the heart of the Father to the worshipper, back to the Father. Therefore for any song, any musical sound, any word or lyrics to translate into worship, it must be inspired by the Holy Spirit and must be for the purpose of giving it all to the Father.

The Role of Music Instruments

Music is the only thing that activates the body soul and spirit at the same time. Music is able to cut through the different realms at the same time. Music has to do with sounds. The core of sound is vibration, released through friction. Friction spiritually is when the forces of God cuts through the forces of darkness and sound from the heart of the Father is release. It is important to know the role of sound or instrument in worship, for they are indeed inspired by God himself. This is why when music gets to a point in worship, healing breaks out and the sick are healed. The sound of heaven turns weakness into strength.

Someone who has been broken and shattered has the tendency to connect to their soul and spirit more from a point where beautiful and divine melody is released and created through them. Here is why deep lyrics and music are drafted in difficult times. Not everyone actually gravitate towards God when there is an abundance of goodness in their lives. Most people tend to move closer to God when things are not going as they should go live. With the creation of music for worship, the worshipper becomes the likeness of God through the attribute of creativity; thereby becoming a creator just like the Lord. The Lord delights when the works of His hands   function functions in creativity. All major instruments of worship require the use of hands, and the Lord delights in seeing the works of His hands worship Him through the works of their hands. This is why God highly abhors evil deeds; when people do evil, they ridicule and taint the works of God's hands.

Worship Music & Warfare

There is nothing that prepares for warfare more than worship songs. As powerful as words are, when words are pulled into songs, there is double declaration in the heavenlies. The entire body, heart and spirit of man and even the bones which is the core of the song begins to move to the melody of the Word joyfully. The individual declare words yet moves and dances along, the entire soul is lifted up and the soul rejoices, fearing nothing. The song conditions the mind of the individual and sets the perfect stage for the divine to come and take over the battle. In spiritual war, joy is a great strategy and weapon - worship songs ahead of warfare makes the entire difference.

The Mystery of the Horns

Before our first ever *Worship Unto Deliverance Event* in 2017, God said to us, prepare a Shofar to be blown during the worship session. We didn't get one before the event. During the event, two women showed up and were sitting right in front. And one of them brought a Shofar. At some point in the ministration, the Lord said, invite her to come and blow the Shofar unto me. And we shared the story of how God had told us to bring Shofar along and even when we fail to, how He has made a brand new way for someone else to bring their Shofar to fulfill His purpose.

Many times after this event, the Lord gave us deeper revelation on the Shofar. Sometimes in 2018, while worship was going on, my husband heard the Lord call me forward to blow the Shofar. After the worship was over, a sister came to ask me; what is this Shofar? what does it mean? and why do you blow it at LightHill? Her questions were valid, especially coming from a person from Africa who has possibly seen movies where satanists invoked curses and spells using horns.

God said, "teach my people about the things I show you". This question brought us into a series of teachings in the Bible Study on Shofar as well as the revelation the Lord gave. The times we shared was coincided with the times of the Holy Feasts of the Lord.

The Shofar

"SHOFAR" is ram's horn and the word comes from the Hebrew language. The Shofar is an instrument of praise and of spiritual warfare. The Shofar will be well explained until we explore the source of the Shofar. Shofar comes from Ram's horn and an adult lamb is called ram. A sheep in its first year is called lamb, so a baby lamb is a sheep. Sheep was first found and reared in the Mesopotamia region before sheep made their way all over the world. The Mesopotamia region in current times covers Iraq, Kuwait, Northern Saudi Arabia, Eastern Syria and parts of Turkey.

Historians have linked these regions to be part of Ur of the Chaldees - Abraham's place of origin Genesis 11:28. And later in Genesis 22:13 - when Abraham was about to sacrifice his only son Isaac to God, he was presented with a ram to be used as sacrifice. Abraham's son represents God's only Son who was used for our sacrifice. A closer look at the history of sheep tells that sheep came from Abraham's home, which was where the angel of God appeared and presented him with the lamb instead of his son.

The Scripture records, as they walked to the site of sacrifice, Isaac asked his father, *"We have the fire and the wood,"* the boy said, *"but where is the sheep for the burnt offering"* in Genesis 22:7 to which Abraham responded, *"Abraham answered, "God himself will provide the lamb for the burnt offering, my son." And the two of them went on together"* - *Genesis 22:8*. Abraham's response was a prophecy that would be fulfilled in the future when Jesus came as flesh into the world as the Lamb of God whom the Father had prepared as a burnt offering. The significance of this prophecy to Abraham's sacrifice is the choice of the animal with is - the lamb. Little did Abraham know he was pre-fulfilling a prophecy that was to come. A prophecy which could not be fulfilled without genuine love for the Lord. This is the nature of the heart of a true worshipper.

The Mystery of the Lamb and the Horn

I was blowing the Shofar and the Lord opened up my mind. What happens when a Lamb shows up in front of you and said, it does not matter how much sin you have on your neck; he'd die for you so you do not have to owe the debt for your sin. The lamb on getting his dead sentence is taken to the slaughter; on its way he didn't say a word. On getting to the slaughter, the lamb went through torture and it began to cry. As I blew the shofar louder and louder, I heard of the cry of a lamb, getting louder and louder. As it got louder, the Lord said to me, "imagine the lamb about to be slaughtered for the sins of the world, yet before the lamb is killed, the world turns back, away from him, not even thinking he was getting killed for their sake. The Lord said to me, "the loud cry you heard was the representation of the cry of the Lord Jesus on the cross and here is the mystery of the horn of salvation.

There is deep mysteries embedded on the shofar, the Shofar is an instrument of warfare and one of the devil's most hated warfare instruments. The Shofar declares the presence of God and the devil fears at the blast of Shofar because he's being reminded that at the coming of the Lord Jesus, the blast of the Shofar will sound and that will declare an end to his reign and mark the beginning of his eternal destruction.

.

Trumpet

The trumpet is another musical instruments found in the presence of God. Trumpets are handed over when there's about to go forth a declaration, warning, announcement, call-to-action, or to invoke certain actions. In times of war, Israel was told to have the priests blow the trumpets. When trumpets are blown, a call for help is sent to heaven and the Lord sends safety to his people.

Trumpets declare the presence of God. When God came down to Mount Sinai, the entire mountain was in smoke, and there was blasting sounds of the trumpet getting louder just before Moses spoke to God and God spoke to him by voice - Exodus 19:19.

The sound of the trumpets will usher in Jesus as He comes in the cloud in his second coming. There will be major 7 trumpets blast at the end of time after Jesus had come and returned with the saints

Wind Instruments

Different instruments play different roles in worship. Wind instruments have a way of connecting to God beyond what others instruments could do. There is no instrument that can fulfill the role of declaration of war in worship other than wind instruments. It is a release of God's breath back to God. And instrument that primarily functions based on the medium of air. It depends solely on the propagation of atmospheric air. A wind instrument will not work in a vacuum. There is always a reason why wind instruments are louder, without any amplification is louder than other instruments. - Because it is the release of the breath of God back to Him. When Moses recounts the revelation of the creation man given to him in Genesis 2:4, after man was formed with the dust, man didn't become a living being until God breathed the breath of life into his nostrils. This is the mystery in worshipping with wind instruments. The worshipper is saying to the Lord; Lord, breath you gave to me, I give it all back to you.

Harp

Harp are instruments found in the presence of God. Each of the 24 elders in heaven hold on to their harps in the worship of God. Harps have been released on earth from way back before the time Cain and Abel, if not Adam and Eve. From the lineage of Cain, there was Juba whom the Scripture described as the father of all those who play the harp and flute in Genesis 4:21. Instruments like the harp is an instrument that beckons to other instruments to come into worship. The grandfather of other instruments like Organs, Keyboard and Guitars. As it releases the sounds, there is a call to other instruments to come join. That is why the keyboard or the harp always sounds as the background where other instruments can build upon. As the sound is being released, the heart of humans hears this and moved into the realm of worship, the realm of worship is the realm of Power and glory where worshippers come together, not interacting physically, but their spirits interacting together as one, to become as one sound and one spirit.

Harps carry a special anointing for revelation. Many worshippers in the company of God are Harpists. Notable harpist in the scripture are the 24 elders, King David and Job, sons of Asaph, Heman, Jeduthun and others like the Israelites who were taken captive in Babylon. There are also harpist and the sounds of many harps around the throne of God in Revelation 14:2. The anointing for powerful revelation is released to the harp, because it is one of the closest instrument to the light and glory of God. This is one of the revelations David had when he said in Psalms 49-4 - *I will incline my ear to a proverb; I will disclose my dark sayings on the harp.* A worshipper is given revelation as they relate and fellowship with their musical instrument. It is like playing with copies of instruments before the throne of God. Because of the so much covenant of revelation upon the harp, the Scripture records that Jeduthun prophesied with the harp in 1 Chronicles 25:3.The powerful sound of the harp can cut overturn the heavenly ordinances and disrupt the flow of night and day David said in Psalm 108:2 *Awake, luke and harp! I will awaken the dawn.* Apostle Paul by revelation said, *"Even if things without life, whether flute or harp, when they make a sound, unless they make a distinction in the sounds, how will it be known that is piped or played? - 1* Corinthians 14:7 - talking about the revelation that comes from the sounds giving the musician the insight and translation into the meaning of sounds.

When the prodigal child picks up to the harp and make sweet melodies to the Lord; he gets the attention of the Lord. The harp is one of the instruments that God has covenanted for the remembrance of his people when they go in repentance in praises. This is one of the mysteries revealed in the book of the Prophet Isaiah 23:16.

Perversion of Music Instruments

The enemy tries to replicate the oneness of sound - when Nebuchadnezzar created an image to be worshipped. He brought in all sorts of instruments and asked all the people of Babylons including the ones who are held captive from Israel to worship him. What this explains is that musical instruments can be perverted and diverted to the use of the devil. Any sound that is not primarily to worship Yahweh is idolatry. Majority of these worldly songs are demonic, originating from the depths of Sheol. Most of these songs are created to bring death to mighty destinies. The sound of the kingdom of darkness weakens strong and great people who are destined for high places in life.

The Talking Drum

Any instrument dedicated to the use of God has the potential to become perverted. There are satanic priests and agents who have mastered the use of drums for wicked acts. Some of them use it to code disaster into people's destiny. In some African ancient towns, there are certain drums made with all sorts of human skin, these drums are rarely beaten, once beaten, trouble is spread en masse. The perversion of drums is so dynamic that there are some families whose traditional occupation is drumming. There are some satanically dedicated drums that can only be played by only groups from this family. Anyone who plays those drums opens themselves up to satanic attacks and the consequences are sometimes grave. Many naive musicians with good intentions unknowing purchase drums made with traditional satanic values and take it to play in local churches. Spirit-filled ministers can discern this and have them put those types of instruments away. Here's more on the perversion of drums from the book - **Uncursed**:,

"*A popular deity with Nigerian roots and has spread to countries like Brazil, Haiti, Trinidad and many countries in America is worshipped with certain type of drum. and when these drums are beaten, demons rejoice in worship of their god. In some families in Africa, especially the royal ones where "princes" and "princesses" are raised. Special demonic drums are beat on special occasion. The sounds of these drums are rooted in the worship of the devil. As the drum is beaten, varieties of demons are released and possess naive listeners and passersby. Some drums are used to wreak havoc in people's live and infiltrate all sorts of evil Whenever the drums are beaten - descendants of certain family lines can be called back home from anywhere in the world. As a young boy, I was privileged to go on experiential trips from school to the ancient town of Ile-Ife where some high-ranking chiefs told them stories of drums. The old man said there were different types of drums; it was said that there were drums made from human skin. There are also some drums tied to some family names"* -

Uncursed
Ebenezer-Gabriels Publishers
Uncursed.Org

African culture employ the heavy use of talking drums. Many of these drums were made with the purpose of idol worship in mind. Drums has a way of getting into the bones when played. When the trumpet is blown, dance styles can be controlled. When the drum is played, the wavelength of sound produced is short and distinct. It has a tendency of moving the body and the bones - rapidly altering people's state. The drum is a great tool for warfare praise. People can get into warfare praise if instruments are consecrated., otherwise people can be led away into self-worship and other types of perverted worship when the wrong instrument is brought in. Self worship is the expression of witchcraft in the church. Self-worship says "Listen to my voice, my voice is awesome and more". The worshipper begins to worship their looks, beauty, and all other things given by God. This has a potential of ruining the worshipper faster than anything. those who come close to me must live in fear and reverence of me. Any worshipper who takes God's glory goes in a state of decline. They may be talented, but they have stolen God's glory. No one can steal God's glory and survive it.

The African Percussion

There are times when witches intentionally bring demonic percussion to destroy the rhythm of the heartbeat of the church, to cause confusion, commotion, and division in the church. From demonic covens, underwaters, they program chants incantations, curses into the creation of those instrument and utter demonic decrees. During worship, they also begin to make sounds to disrupt the move of God, with a foreign object infested with demons. Some of them succeed if the church is not in the right spiritual standing before God. The evil goal behind this is to chase the gathering out of God's presence by mixing a strange fire into the worship of God's people - knowing that God will not take any unholy worship.

Out of all the musical instruments, the drum is the most perverted and certain groups of people have incorporated drums into idolatry. This why some assemblies stay away completely from the use of drums. This is not popular, but it is what it is.

Demonic Music

Back in the autumn of 2017, my eyes were opened up to a revelation. In that revelation, I saw a body cream on display and the Lord said the cream originated from a polluted source. We shared in our gathering the revelation. A few weeks later; someone sent us a published news about a body cream. The Research Specialist who worked in production of the lotion passed away and no one else was able to get the formula of the lotion in the company. The cream was one of the best selling products of the company. One of the researchers suggest a fix. They consulted a medium who helped them beckon to the spirit of the dead researcher. The spirit of the dead gave the formula, and included as part of the recipe was a special music playing in the background while the formula is being mixed. The formula was got right and the cream went back into the market. There are a lot of these versions of polluted products in the market today.

The role of music is not hidden in the kingdom of darkness. Here is what Kingdom citizens must be aware that music cuts through different realms and the intake of polluted music can marr destinies forever. There are a lot of demonic music that flows into the bones. Many are addicted to these music, not knowing the foundation of these songs. In glorying these music, listeners are worshipping the creator of such music which is the devil. Demonic music is one of the ways for the enemy to penetrate the core of the masses There is a faster way that the demonic locks and seals up people in dormant curses - this is through satanic music. There are some type of curses which are laying dormant in the lives of people without them even knowing. Demonic music are created from covens and sent into the world, most of these are saturated in clubs, public places. When these music are played into the hearing of many, certain curses become activated and people get locked down. Music carries such great power because it has the ability to cut across the realms of the body, spirit and soul at the same time - hence it's able to transport and transfer demons faster.

29

WORSHIP, MUSIC & THE PROPHETIC

PROPHETIC IN WORSHIP

> *"Then another angel, having a golden censer, came and stood at the altar. He was given much incense, that he should offer it with the prayers of all the saints upon the golden altar which was before the throne. And the smoke of the incense, with the prayers of the saints, ascended before God from the angel's hand".*

> **REVELATION 8:3-4 NKJV**

The prophet Elisha had received the double portion of the spirit and power of the Prophet Elijah. This means he could decree that the heavens be close up that it wouldn't rain for 3 years and also pray that it would rain at His command. The horsepower of the fire of the Holy Spirit in Him could defeat more prophets of baal than Elijah did. In his prophetic career, there were many prophetic successful works. Prophet Elisha chased out the spirit of death from the water source, works, there were financial miracles, healing miracles, and the dead brought back to life.

During his career, there came a time where Elisha's life opens up the mystery of the connectivity of worship music and the prophetic. When King Joram - the King of Israel, Ahab and Jezebel's son sought to inquire of the Lord concerning a war Israel was engaged in with the king of Moab. The king Joram and Israel army together with supporters like King Jehosaphat of Judah were already in some form of trouble and they needed to hear from God.

2 King 3:11-15

But King Jehoshaphat of Judah asked, "Is there no prophet of the Lord with us? If there is, we can ask the Lord what to do through him." One of King Joram's officers replied, "Elisha son of Shaphat is here. He used to be Elijah's personal assistant." Jehoshaphat said, "Yes, the Lord speaks through him." So the king of Israel, King Jehoshaphat of Judah, and the king of Edom went to consult with Elisha.

When they located Elisha. Elisha was still fighting the war of worship though Elijah had gone. Elisha told the king of Israel that he would not had granted him audience but for the sake of Jehoshaphat, the King of Judah who was present.

."Why are you coming to me?" Elisha asked the king of Israel. "Go to the pagan prophets of your father and mother!" But King Joram of Israel said, "No! For it was the Lord who called us three kings here—only to be defeated by the king of Moab!" Elisha replied, "As

243

surely as the Lord Almighty lives, whom I serve, I wouldn't even bother with you except for my respect for King Jehoshaphat of Judah. Now bring me someone who can play the harp." While the harp was being played, the power of the Lord came upon Elisha.

God's presence is rare; anyone who gets into God's presence does not get there without a cost. Elisha the Prophet needed to hear from Heaven. He needed to divine the heart of God. Tuning your mind to anointed sounds does the work of realignment to purpose and destiny and can open up the realm of the prophetic. The mind can decipher the encryption embedded into music unbeknown to the musician. There are encryption of sounds and of old sayings embedded in music. The mind can translate these encryption. That's why king David said, *"I will utter my dark sayings on the harp"*. An anointed worshipper carries the word of God in their heart - when music is created with their instruments; the word of God in them mixes with the sound of their music, holy and anointed, the Holy Spirit takes over the musician, leading them all the way to capture the sound of heaven and bring into the moment.

Prophet Elisha needed the oil flowing from an anointed musician. He wouldn't just bring an entertainer or a desecrated musician, but one who was consecrated and anointed, and graced to go into the heavenlies to bring down to the earth, the sound in God's presence. The role of the prophetic musician is to create the sound of heaven. The sound of heaven is what goes before the release of the prophetic. As they brought the minstrel to Prophet Elisha, worship flowed and the sounds of heaven were released. had to come through that worship. Worship is broad. There is a special place for music in worship. Anointed music can get people faster to God's presence

Music & The Prophetic

Worship music and the prophetic has always gone hand in hand. There is no prophetic without a heart of worship, and there is no worshipper without revelation. Revelation comes to the heart of the worshipper, as the mind of the worshipper syncs to the heart of Yahweh.

Minstrels & Worship

An anointed musician who lives in holiness is like a beautiful bride, dressed gloriously waiting for the marriage supper of the Lamb. On the other side, a worshipper who lives outside of holiness becomes wretched, poor, blind and naked in the soul..

Holiness: Anointed musicians are supposed to be individuals who live a life of consecration, and chase after heaven, such that, whenever they set their instruments to play unto the Lord, the breath of God is released. W/he that breath is tainted, they are releasing an expression from the flesh and that will go now where before God.

Revelation: An anointed musician is granted a very rare privilege of the kingdom of God. Generational revelations are unsealed to the anointed musician. When all the priests were going to seek the face of God and wait on the Lord's instruction overnight, King David will sit still in the presence of God, playing harp and divine mysteries of the Lord in generations to come were being revealed to David. Mysteries of God are only opened up to worshippers. Only a circumsized worshipper can find the deep things of God through the power of the Holy Spirit. Only a worshipper can truly live in their purpose; because God has carefully hidden the purpose of everyone;

Humility: The worshipper cannot be separated from humility. Humility is one of the most visible traits of a worshipper. You cannot be miss Great humility. Where there is humility, it is more likely that God is close by. Without humility, God is very far from it. There is no pride that will get into God's presence. No unbrokeness will lead others into God's presence.

Soul: The state of soul of the minstrel is vital and can make or break worship. In the soul of a musician, there is the breath of God. If the breath of God is being nurtured in holiness, and watered with the Word, the air flowing through the pipes of the musician who plays music instruments is considered as releasing God's breathe back to Him in worship.

There is no musician working under the spirit of lust that will ever bring anyone let alone the congregation into the presence of God.

Worth: Anyone who doesnt know worth cannot understand God's worth and worship God. One of the things that can be off in worship is the absence of worth. Those who lack worth are the ones who lack the understanding of the value placed upon their lives by God. Without worth, there is no way a person will worship the God who placed a value - this is not the same as those who started from scratch growing into knowing God. A worshipper must live a life worthy of God's praise. A worshipper must understand their worth in is Jesus and must not be like those who are cover insecurity up with flamboyance, using money to polish external appearance. People who do not understand the worth will not be able to worship God, because they will seek refuge in other gods as a form of protection. They will sing songs about what they have, what they bought, what they used money for. All that is far away from the worship of God. This is why the Scripture say, deep calls unto deep.. Anyone who is not in the understanding of worth cannot worship God. The worship of God is tied to self-worth.The understanding of God's wrath is incremental. The revelation of worship is also incremental. When the angels get a new revelation, all they utter is "holy". One word that can only define God is "holy", hence the angels repeatedly worship Him as more of His glory is revealed to them. Anyone who does not appreciate the side shown by God cannot move forward to another side of God. Anyone who cannot give thanks for the simple things cannot unlock God's revelation. When there is understanding of the worth of being God's worshipper, appreciation is not shown, and revelation is sealed because the glory of God is not for waste.

Worship & Wages: Any musician who collects money to offer a service of worship to God cannot lead others into God's presence. Minstrels can be appreciated, blessed especially when flight costs, hotel costs are involved - however, a worshipper must not go into ministration in an assembly with the mindset of rendering a service and getting paid for such service. Only a few people can isolate the music service they offer in God's house for payment and worship they offer to God. Ministering for money soils the worship, because there is a god of Mammon accepting the worship. The devil is tainting worship from the churches, especially from the area of worship. The pastors place the worship musicians as top of the line workers, offering them a higher pay scale than the other sanctuary workers who are paid. The musicians are treated with care and sometimes worshipped for the fear of not losing. For some of these reasons, the Church has lost the power and favor of God.These things do not go with worship:

30

WORSHIP & THE HOLY SPIRIT

KING DAVID'S DESIRE TO BUILD GOD'S HOUSE

> *Now it came to pass when the king was dwelling in his house, and the Lord had given him rest from all his enemies all around, that the king said to Nathan the prophet, "See now, I dwell in a house of cedar, but the ark of God dwells inside tent curtains.*
>
> **2 SAMUEL 7:1-2 NKJV**

Worship is communion with the Holy Spirit. Worship cannot take place in the flesh. Worship can only occur within the perimeters of truth and the Holy Spirit. Without the baptism of the Holy Spirit, true worship cannot take place. Any worship that takes place without being directed by the Holy Spirit is worship led by flesh, and is a worship directed to the ruler of this world. The Spirit of Yahweh, the Holy Spirit is the conductor of every worship that ascends into the Father's presence and that is accepted by the Father. Who best to direct worship than the spirit of God Himself? For the Holy Spirit to lead us far in worship, the right proportion of the word of the Lord must be present in us. The spirit of God in man is strengthened with the word of God, adequate time spent in prayers and worship. The working of the power of the Holy Ghost is like a sponge, feeding on water. When the sponge is dry, it becomes hard and cannot absorb. The word of God is an enabler of the Holy Spirit in worship and the word of God must not be lacking in the worshipper, otherwise they would not get far in worship.In worship, the Holy Spirit is like the vehicle and the word of God is the gas in the vehicle, while the worshipper is the willing and submitted passenger in the vehicle. The Holy Spirit functions at his optimal level when the worshipper has in them sufficient word of God in them.

In a worship taking place in truth and in the spirit, the spirit of God is in accord with the spirit of man. There is unison. The heart of the spirits begins to beat together as one. Synchronized with the heartbeat of God and the desire of God becomes the desire of man. The rhythm of the heartbeat of God is totally subscribed to the rhythm of the heartbeat of God. This is where the will of God reflects in the deeds of man.

Themes of Worship

The conductor of worship, the Holy Spirit, releases fresh revelations from the heart of the Father. Each worship session has a divine theme. The worship theme is the current subject of worship the Holy Spirit is ministering to you at the moment. God is highly relational. When you are graced with access into His presence, the spirit of the Lord shares the theme of the moment with the worshipper in heaven.

In a spirit-filled worship team, when the worshippers gather together for a worship meeting, they soon realize that from the time they begin the opening prayer, there is a united flow of communication being received in the spirit. When the praise of the Most High is going on, the angels of God tremble because there is always a new revelation every time. There is no single time that you worship the Lord in the truth and spirit that He doesn't open up newer revelations. This is why a worshipper must never go into worship full of themself. Assuming to know the ways of God throws the worshipper out of God's presence. The worshipper must never ever get familiar with God, thinking they know His ways because He releases revelation to them in the place of worship.

The Place of Fear

There is a place in worship called the place of fear. When you worship to a level, deep fear from God will come down. Once that happens, a different realm is unlocked. This place of fear in worship is referenced in Proverbs 9:10 -*The fear of the LORD is the beginning of wisdom, and knowledge of the Holy One is understanding.* The worshipper gets to a place where the fear of the Lord overshadows them in worship, the Lord meets them with love and revelation. The realm of love and revelation in the place of worship is the where the fear of God is found. A worshipper who lives in the depth fear of God will be able to get beyond the surface of worship. Without the fear of God, there is no worship. This is the point God begins to share His heart with His worshippers. In this realm, the place of His fear, is a place of honoring God and having deeper communion with Him. It is the place where an expansion is granted to the mind of the worshipper because the worshipper is allowed to partake in the fruit from the tree of wisdom in the presence of the Lord. What follows is empowerment, enablement, might and power upon the worshipper to bring the glory of God to the earth.

Knowing that a worshipper fears Him and they will take it upon themselves to be good stewards of His words. Worshippers understand the value of God's word, they understand the value of revelation. They understand it costs so much to get into the presence of God; when they have God's presence, they never want to lose it. They also hold tight to every one of God's words, understanding that there is no price for knowing but there is a price for taking actions.

The Worshiper's Privilege: Heaven's Innovation Room

The early worshippers were the only selected individuals that were given access into the realm of the Holy Spirit. Abraham was given access into revelations of things to come and Noah was given revelation into the things to come. David was also given deeper revelations and had the Holy Spirit abiding with Him long before the birth of His descendant, Jesus. In 2016, the Lord showed me a vision; in that vision I was taken to a major room of inventions in heaven. The place is called the "Innovation Room of Heaven". I was told the room is where all types of inventions are stored. This invention facility of God is well guarded, so that the enemies of God will not get in. There were a lot of angelic guards. It takes people who can give God their whole heart in worship to gain entry. The only people allowed access into that room are those who are given to a life of worship. I saw a lot of musical instruments that we had never seen on earth before. Access to this room is granted only to those whose hearts are sold completely to the Lord in worship. This explains why worshippers tend towards creativity. Since worship has no language and it could be expressed in songs, in writing, in research, in skills, in cooking, sewing, and in all walks of life , the worshiper is blessed in creativity, and ability to invent new songs, writings, recipes, technology, godly arts, crafts and in any field they find themselves. There is a special innovation and creativity available to worshippers. The more they worshipper, the deeper they get into innovation and the more they bring forth to the world.

Worship & Revelation

There's no other person that the Lord would want to reveal Himself and His glory to is not his worshippers. Psalm 49:4 - *I'll incline my ear to a proverb: I will disclose my dark sayings on the harp.* Proverbs are not lighted word, a lot of secrets is buried in a proverb. A lot of directions is hidden in proverbs, and that's why proverbs seem to have multiple meanings. A proverb can be translated wrongly. The one who is given a proverb May search for meaning and never arrive at it. They may rely on men to translate but all get it wrong. Many information the Lord passes to us is encrypted. It is encrypted so that it doesn't get into the wrong hands. Only a worshipper can draw out their meanings. The harp being an instrument of worship. Whatever your tool of worship is, When Job went through his season of affliction, and God responded to him for the first time; God said, Who is this who darkens counsel??? Darkened counsel, darkened information, darkened understanding means confusion.

When worship goes on, the Lord opens up pathways unto people. When worship is going on, the Lord opens up pathway, many just look into that door and take a peak, instead of walking into it, they just close the door. Worshippers who are patient to hold unto God's presence through extreme focus on the word of God and the vastness of the Lord is taken into a pool of revelation into the glory of the Lord and this is only the beginning of the journey. Worship is the journey into the mind of God. As you worship, the way opens to the mind of the Lord and He begins to take people to the depth of His mind. A lot is available in worship. When the spirit of God in man is in accord with the spirit of man. There is unison. The heart of the spirits begin to beat together as one. Synchronized with the heartbeat of God and the desire of God becomes the desire of man. The rhythms of the heartbeat of God because man is totally subscribed to the rhythm of the heartbeat of God. This is where the will of God reflects in the deeds of man.

Worship and Light

Worship is associated with associated with the quietness of the spirit. That is why often times people close their eyes when they are in deep worship. The closing of eyes in deep worship talks about the absence of distraction. Although it is not equally or mutually exclusive, people can still close their eyes and imagine vain things. When people close their eyes they want to be free of distraction, they are shutting out the physical distractions. It is what many houses of worship tries to replicate by turning out the light or deeming the light. Although a lot of people misuse this because they do not understand this. When people worship and there is the absence of very harsh light, there is focus.The Holy Spirit is not hindered by the absence or presence of light. It is the Holy Spirit who is the light illuminates the hearts of men. It is so interesting that men try to close their eyes and shut their eyes so that their hearts can be illuminated.

In places where evangelism needs to go on, you cannot have the lights turned off. The evangelistic gospel needs to go straight into the eyes. It is not something that needs to be imagined, it is something that needs to be known. In the realm of worship, it is about cutting off distractions. Some have indeed taken it to the other way. Some lights are the equivalence of disco lights, in trying to cut off they have introduced distractions.

Beyond all the lights, the heart that is seeking after God will know how to shut out every distraction. Afterall a heart that is not saved when they close their eyes, what they see is not His presence.

31

WORSHIP AS A LIFESTYLE

THE IDENTITY OF WORSHIP

> *"The spirit of a man is the lamp of the LORD, Searching all the inner depths of his heart."*
>
> **PROVERBS 20:27**

Worship is beyond songs and dance, it is the way we live, it is the way we do our jobs, the way we study, the way we cook, the way we act, the way we think. Worship can be integrated into all that we do.

The Identity of Worship

There is uniqueness in everything God has created, including worship. Scientists have discovered that the fingerprint pattern is unique to every individual, and far beyond the fingerprint, there are other unique elements in the human body. The iris pattern is unique such that no two eyes have the same pattern, not even identical twins. The tongue patterns is also unique, the human voice, vein patterns in the palm, retina, and finger are all unique also unique to every individual. This is one of the mysteries of God - creating each and every one of us to be unique and distinct. Proverbs 20:27 says, *"The spirit of a man is the lamp of the LORD, Searching all the inner depths of his heart."* Scientists have employed a similar method to what we find in Proverbs 20:27 such that a special type of light is harnessed to scanning devices to recognize unique patterns in fingerprints, veins, iris and other parts of the human body. This technique used for identification in science was derived from the Proverb 20:27 Scripture. This scripture gives us a peek into how God has placed a special type of light in all humans through His spirit, to search out the content of the human heart and present updates back to God.

The same concept is seen in worship. Worship has an identity. Each person's worship has a unique identifier before God. This is why some worship goes before the Lord as a sweet smelling aroma and why others go as a stench, hence rejected. The altar of worship in the human vessel is the heart. Inside humans is the lamp of God, examining the heart. This is why when certain people begin to worship, the host of heaven rejoice and say, "this worshipper has come again" and they open up heaven. The same reason is why another person begins to offer worship, the angels shut the doors of heaven because of the odor oozing out of the heart of the perverse worshipper.

Worship carries different tags. There is a detail in every worship. Majority of things classified as worship is not worship because it is not intentional. Without a person being intentional about their worship to God, worship becomes accidental and accidental worship cannot go far. Intentional worship began from the heart of God is released to a particular soul through the spirit of God - they get to the place of worshipping God deeply. The spouse could join that part of worship. It was not intentional for the spouse, but was accidental for the spouse. One could be drawn into what was not their original plan - it has been decreed and ordained by the sovereign Lord. Intentail worship is when one puts their heart towards everything they are doing. Eating and glorifying God over the food they eat. Whatever is not renewed has the tendency to carry complacency. International worship comes with a heart of worship. Praise is verbal. Worship is the state of the soul, it is the state of the heart, it could be verbal, but deeper than what could be uttered by the lips. Worship can produce a radical state in the psychology and emotions of man that it produces tears. When certain chemical changes happen in the body, it translates into tears. When the spirit of God moves inside of man, it not only stays in the spirit, it enters into the soul, and the soul communicates with the body and the body reacts chemically. Worship is the activity that transcends between realms, the spirit, soul and the body.

Research as Worship

When humans worship God for the works of His hands. A lot of people do not realize how much the Father delights in people using their divine giftings. As a writer, you can worship God through your writings. There are deep and engaging writers, writers who write as though they copy the mind of God. Writers whose content delights God, because the content originates from Him in the first place.

There are researchers who worship the Lord through their research and Psalms 111:2 confirms, saying - *The LORD's works are great, studied by all who delight in them.* God loves research. He keeps things hidden and wants us to research and find them out. This is why the Scripture says in Proverbs 25:2 - *It is the glory of God to conceal a thing: but the honour of kings is to search out a matter.* A worshipper is given a mind of research. A heart that is curious about the works of God and a worshipper appreciates more.

In our short time of walking with and working for the Lord, we have been privileged to encounter God as the *"Lord who hides Himself"* as the Prophet Isaiah stated in Isaiah 45:15.
This is why only a few truly work through purpose in their lifetime because research has been neglected by many and only a few go the tedious way of research. Innovation is born from the place of worshipping the Lord for the works of His hands. When people worship the Lord for His creations, the Lord begins to open up the eyes of their understanding into His creation. He begins to show them the hidden treasures in His creations. He gives them more information about that creation that has not been released to anyone, because anyone has never bothered to ask. In academia, this is the sphere of doctoral research. A major purpose a person in pursuit of a Ph.D is to research into an area and extract out new and valuable information to contribute to an existing knowledge bank. This is the privilege of a worshipper.

When Buzz Aldrin opted to go into the military, it started with a heart willing to serve His nation. Then as he mastered his role and skills, he sought further knowledge and obtained a doctorate degree in Astronautics. Little did he know that together with his commander, they would be granted a safe return trip into another celestial body and his findings will bring scholars to a new understanding leading them to rewrite textbooks on the Moon and the solar system.

In preparation for the flight to the moon, each pilot had an only a few personal allowance to take onboard. Aldrin traded other choice personal belongings for : a *Bible verse written on a slip of paper, a bread wafer, a small amount of wine and a tiny silver chalice* - which he was given to him by his pastor. He took the communion to the moon and planned to join his church *"as close as possible to the same hour"* in having the communion, and *"meaning to represent in this small way not only our local church but the Church as a whole"*. in his words:

> *"Houston, this is Eagle. This is the LM Pilot speaking. I would like to request a few moments of silence. I would like to invite each person listening in, wherever and whomever he may be, to contemplate for a moment the events of the past few hours and to give thanks in his own individual way." For me this meant taking communion. In the radio blackout I opened the little plastic packages which contained bread and wine. I poured the wine into the chalice our church had given me. In the one-sixth gravity of the moon the wine curled slowly and gracefully up the side of the cup. It was interesting to think that the very first liquid ever poured on the moon, and the first food eaten there, were communion elements. And so, just before I partook of the elements, I read the words which I had chosen to indicate our trust that as man probes into space we are in fact acting in Christ. I sensed especially strongly my unity with our church back home, and with the Church everywhere. I read: "I am the vine, you are the branches. Whoever remains in me, and I in him, will bear much fruit; for you can do nothing without me." John 15:5 (TEV)*

Because of Aldrin's heart given to worship, the first meal to served and eaten on the moon was the elements of the Holy Communion, representing the body and the blood of Jesus Christ - with the worshipper not forgetting to to partake in unity and love at almost the same time with his church gathering located about an average of 238,855 miles away , which is about 30 Earths away. He didn't shy away from his faith and moment of worship, he broadcasted the Holy Communion Service to the flight team back in earth. Aldrin and Armstrong had the understanding that their mission to the moon was based on the prior research work of about 300 to 400 thousand people and the entire America and humanity had high hopes in their findings. Aldrin communed with the Lord quoting the words of John 15:5 *I am the vine, you are the branches. Whoever remains in me, and I in him, will bear much fruit; for you can do nothing without me.*

After His mission on the moon, having been privileged to see the works of God outside of this planet.

Marriage As Worship

Marriage is the prophetic copy of the relationship between Jesus and the Church. The day of wedding being a replica of what is to come at the marriage supper of the Lamp. Marriage is worship, according to God's plan. When John encountered the revelation of what was to come at the Marriage Supper, his only response was to worship.

Revelation 19:6-10 NKJV

And I heard, as it were, the voice of a great multitude, as the sound of many waters and as the sound of mighty thunderings, saying, "Alleluia! For the Lord God Omnipotent reigns! Let us be glad and rejoice and give Him glory, for the marriage of the Lamb has come, and His wife has made herself ready." And to her it was granted to be arrayed in fine linen, clean and bright, for the fine linen is the righteous acts of the saints. Then he said to me, "Write: 'Blessed are those who are called to the marriage supper of the Lamb!' " And he said to me, "These are the true sayings of God." And I fell at his feet to worship him. But he said to me, "See that you do not do that! I am your fellow servant, and of your brethren who have the testimony of Jesus. Worship God! For the testimony of Jesus is the spirit of prophecy."

Marriage was created to worship the Lord. The marriage

institution can be looked at as a form of church; the gathering and fellowship of God's people within a family unit. Here is why the greatest opposition and threat against marriages is the gates of Hades.

The marriage is a copy of the relationship between Jesus and the Church. The husband is the priest of the Lord in the house, bringing his wife and children before the Lord. The wife is the Shepherd, assisting in the building and management of the family.

As no church will stand without a living altar for God, a marriage without the altar of God will not stand. There are many worship ministers, leaders of congregation, teachers, prophets, prophetess who lead gatherings at worship events, but worship is missing from their marriages. Many husbands who will not submit to the ordinance of the Lord, and has lost their godly authority over their families - yet without submission to the Lord, they lead congregations. There are wives who have torn their spouses down with their mouths and have drained the essence of life out of their families with their tongues, yet they go to lead people in worship at gatherings.

The Spirit & Curse of Eve

When satan attempts to pervert worship across the land, he looks for a vulnerable family as he did with Adam and Eve. Worship is obedience to the words and the ways of God. The enemy has brought his own perverted principles of marriage into the world and many have adopted - rejecting the ordinance of God in marriage. The curse of Eve at work in the life of women is to lead men away from the worship of Yahweh. By default, Abrahm had been obeying God before Eve was created. Eve had fallen and become disobedient and dragged Adam into dishonoring God. The curse of Eve can be at work through the spirit empowering that curse and be operational in the life of man or woman. The curse of Eve is genderless. It is solely responsible for luring worshippers into disobedience to God and honoring satan instead, thereby chasing them out of God's presence.

Unfortunately, the spirit of Eve is usually close to home to worshippers. The spirit finds a person very close to the ministry like the Pastor's wife, Prophet's wife, minister's mother and use them to chase worshippers out of God's presence. The spirit of Eve that is not defeated will grow into the spirit of Jezebel that will pervert the worship of an entire nation.

33

A CALL TO WORSHIP

WORSHIP IN THE EARTHLY SANCTUARY

> " *Do you not know that your bodies are temples of the Holy Spirit, who is in you, whom you have received from God? You are not your own; you were bought at a price. Therefore honor God with your bodies.*"
>
> **1 CORINTHIANS 6:19-20**

The Vision of the Deer & The Lion

There is a strong bond between the deer and water. The best way to capture the attention of a deer is to provide them with water. David understood this and said to God in Psalm 42:1 - *As the deer longs for streams of water, so I long for you, O God.*

The Lord opened my eyes and I saw a vision of the congregation of deer running to the brook of water. As they were running to the water, there were also a lot of lions and wolves, devouring them and some of them were not able to get to the water. I asked the Lord for the meaning of this revelation and He said this is what is happening to people who have stood up for Jesus in the

261

Middle East and some other dark places of the world. Places where accepting to walk in righteousness means not only enmity with family, but departure from the world. As people discover the light of the gospel and become thirsty for His word, thrusting and longing for the King of kings, the radical enemy comes to take their lives away for boldly moving on to the righteous side. There are some people who were able to get to the source of water, into a place of God's presence to worship God. The question is, will your soul long for Him? Will you thirst for Him?

A Call to Worship

When the message of salvation was preached to us, it was an invitation to a to worship, a proposal to become the bride of the Son of God and Jesus was saying to us: Deep in my heart I have loved. I have made a banquet for you. Your sins are forgiven, I have paid the price with my blood, will you marry me? The Father has chosen the date of the wedding, will you marry me because I have great love you. These are the words of Jesus, calling to worship the Lord through a union with Him. What love is greater than the love that made one pay the debt of another with his blood?

How Does One Become a Worshipper?

A person becomes a worshipper by understating what it means to be a worshipper, by understanding the ways of life of worshipper, and get to a point where they introduce worship into every facet of their life. A person who has been a mindless engineer, after they realize what worship is and that each line of code they write is worship unto God and they do it differently.

34

THE WORSHIPPER'S PRAYER

WORSHIP IN THE EARTHLY SANCTUARY

> *" Do you not know that your bodies are temples of the Holy Spirit, who is in you, whom you have received from God? You are not your own; you were bought at a price.Therefore honor God with your bodies."*
>
> **1 CORINTHIANS 6:19-20**

The war of disinformation is a war that started by the kingdom of darkness. The goal is to bombard the believers with incorrect information, woven from the pit of hell and lead them out of God's laws. Satan constructs things that look like the word of God and get His agents to distribute false information. There are many cliches that are the fabrication of the heart of men. After fully circulating the information, people believe that they do not bother to check the Scriptures. This is how worship was perverted originally.

Having read through the length of the pages in this book, you may be wondering, how do I worship God and where do I begin since there is no template for worship. There is a safe place to start, a place where the worshipper declare the attributes of God back to God in prayers and in the word of God. Many ask; how to pray these prayers, extolling the names of God.

There is no intentional worshipper of God who does not hear the voice of the Lord. The Lord will speak. Often times, people blanket everything into worship.. one must be intentional about it.

The Prayer of the Worshipper's

The worshipper's prayer is the prayer of beckoning to the Lord from His attributes as revealed by the Scriptures. This is when a worshipper declare God's praises back to Him; it is a way to petition God from a heart with an intent to worship. For anyone who intends to worship God and does not know where to begin or what to say; you can start to utter words that describe the attributes of God, back to God.

Appealing to the Awesome attribute of God

No one qualifies for the title of "Awesome" here on earth. The word "awesomeness" is fear provoking. Whenever a worshipper gets before the Lord with their whole mind, and they say "you are the awesome God". They are beckoning to the awesomeness of God and instances where God displays Himself as awesome.

The Prayer of the Worshipper:

To appeal to the **awesomeness of God**

> God, you are the awesome majesty
> You are the Most High who is awesome
> Your name is great and awesome
> You who did awesome things by the Red Sea
> You are known for the might of your awesome acts,
> You show yourself as awesome in all your doings.
> How awesome are the works of your hands

Lord, you are more awesome than your holy places
All your deeds are awesome
You are the One and Only Awesome One
The awesome God who keeps every covenant

The prayer of the worshipper:
To appeal to the **holiness of God**

You who have sworn by your holiness
You adorn your house with holiness
You have called us into the beauty of holiness
You speak and utter words in holiness
You are glorious in holiness
Holiness belongs to you and your foundation is in the holy mountains
Holy are you, o Lord of the heavenly host
Your promises are holy
Your Sabbath is holy
Your spirit o'Lord, is the Holy Spirit.

The prayer of the worshipper:
To appeal to the **excellency of God**

God, your excellency is over Israel
You overthrow your enemies in your excellence
Your name is excellent and awesome
You are excellent in power, honor and glory
In all your doings you are excellent and mighty
You are great in excellence
All across the earth, your name is the most excellent
Your spirit o Lord, is that of excellence

REFERENCES

Chapter 21 – Worships as a Lifestyle

https://www.houstonchronicle.com/local/space/mission-moon/article/Church-of-the-Astronauts-Webster-church-13766755.php#photo-17226423

https://www.guideposts.org/better-living/life-advice/finding-life-purpose/guideposts-classics-when-buzz-aldrin-took-communion-on-the-moon?_ga=2.254347656.1601112826.1565716704-860397664.1565716704

ABOUT THE AUTHORS

Ebenezer Gabriels is an anointed Prophet, Worship Minister, Deliverance Minister and Intercessor for the nations. Abigail is a Pastor, Bible Teacher, Minstrel & Intercessor.
Ebenezer Gabriels Ebenezer and Abigail worship together gifted technologists and have worked extensively in the areas of Computing and Data science.

Ebenezer and Abigail are involved in Church planting, were used the Pastors of LightHill Church - A worship-focused church USA. They are also involved in strategic 6-hour worship and national intercession movements. Their mandate is to revive worship altars and intercede for nations. Ebenezer is married to Abigail, and their lives are a testimony of the resurrection power and worship of the Lord

EGƎ
Ebenezer Gabriels Ministries

ABOUT EGM

EGM provides resources for people to encounter Jesus. Our mandate is to revive dead worship altars, uproot rottenness from foundations, release God's people into Yahweh's worship, and intercede for the nations.

EGM's arm of publishing designs and develops Christian resources inspired by the Lord. EGM currently operates out of Gaithersburg in Maryland, USA.

CONTACT

Office/Mailing
19644 Club House Road Suite 815, Gaithersburg, Maryland, 20876 USA

hello@ebenezergabriels.org
www.ebenezergabriels.org

OTHER BOOKS BY EBENEZER & ABIGAIL GABRIELS

DEEPER MYSTERIES

OF THE

SOUL

Ebenezer Gabriels
Abigail Gabriels

UNCURSED

A PROPHETIC BOOK TO RAISE A CURSELESS GENERATION

Features
BACK-TO-THE-Womb
deliverance prayers

Prayers before, during &
after pregnancy

Prayers for babies in the
womb
And more

Ebenezer Gabriels
Abigail Gabriels

RAPID FIRE

Apostolic prayers that evoke heaven's swift response to major spiritual attacks.

Ebenezer & Abigail
Gabriels

WISDOM

My Companion

A transformative 7-day devotional

Ebenezer & Abigail Gabriels

HEROD

The CHURCH & NIGERIA

Beckoning the Church into Repentance, Humility & Intercession for
Stability in the Times of the Soon-to-begin Persecution

Ebenezer Gabriels
Abigail Gabriels

THE SCROLL
&
THE SEAL

NIGERIA

A DESECRATED NATION WITH A PROPHETIC DESTINY

The Role of the Church, 2019 Elections & the Upcoming Revival

Ebenezer Gabriels
Abigail Gabriels

www.ingramcontent.com/pod-product-compliance
Lightning Source LLC
Chambersburg PA
CBHW060011100426
42740CB00010B/1452